VIRAL CRITIQUE: BIOARZTCHY AGAINST BIOPOTENCY IN THE COVID-19 AGE

Viral Critique: Bioarztchy Against Biopotency in the COVID-19 Age

Andityas Soares de Moura Costa Matos

Francis García Collado

Translation from Portuguese by
Andityas Soares de Moura Costa Matos and Gregorio Menzel

COUNTERPRESS
OXFORD

First published 2022
Counterpress, Oxford
http://counterpress.org.uk

© 2022 Andityas Soares de Moura Costa Matos and Francis García Collado

Rights to publish and sell this book in print, electronic, and all other forms and media are exclusively licensed to Counterpress Limited. An electronic version of this book is available under a Creative Commons Attribution-NonCommercial (CC-BY-NC 4.0) International license via the Counterpress website:

https://counterpress.org.uk

ISBN: 978-1-910761-15-1 (Paperback)
ISBN: 978-1-910761-16-8 (ePDF)

Typeset in 10.5 on 12pt Sabon

Cover art by Desali (desali_xo on instagram and desali.com)

Global print and distribution by Ingram

We dedicate this book to all health professionals that, resisting the seduction of the bioarztchy, engaged themselves in a modest and anonymous parrhesia act by taking care of our lives and risking theirs.

Acknowledgments

Writing this book in the midst of a pandemic in places as different as Brazil and Spain was a painful and dangerous intellectual adventure, especially since almost nothing is clearly and permanently defined in relation to COVID-19, whether in the scientific, political and philosophical sphere. Therefore, we can only thank with real joy our first editors in Spain (Bellaterra edicions) and Brazil (GLAC edições), who with us gambled on an endeavour that now reaches a wider audience in English with Counterpress. We effusively thank our patient English editor Illan Wall. We owe to Illan's rigorous and careful reading the fact that this version is very different from the original text, incorporating even more contemporary themes and giving us the opportunity to deepen certain discussions only indicated in the books in Spanish and in Portuguese. We also thank Andreas Philippopoulos-Mihalopoulos, whose generosity is already proverbial among his friends and collaborators, who spared no effort to see the book published in English and was responsible for our happy meeting with Counterpress. Finally, we thank our Spanish and Brazilian readers, who surprised us with an excellent reception of this work, to which we hope to soon add our English-speaking companions.

Contents

Introduction 1
    CORONAVIRUS: THANOS' DREAM

1. First Pandemic Philosophy 7
    AGAMBEN, NANCY, ESPOSITO, ŽIŽEK, BUTLER, HAN, PRECIADO,
    BIFO, BADIOU, COCCIA, AND MBEMBE

2. Between the Living and the Non-living 17
    WHAT IS A VIRUS?

3. Beyond the Opposition of Nature and Culture 25
    EVENT, INTRUSION OF GAIA AND ANTHROPOCENE

4. Control of the Pandemic 32
    THE EUROPEAN SOVEREIGN MODEL AND THE ASIAN ALGORITHMIC
    MODEL

5. The Thanatopolitical and Necropolitical Responses of
    Bioarztchy 40
    FEAR AND GOVERNMENTALITY IN THE PANDEMIC

6. Biopotency and Bioemergence 56
    MUTATING TO SUR/VIVE

Conclusion 67
    WHAT HAPPENED TO THE FUTURE? IT WILL NEVER BE LIKE BEFORE

References 70

About the Authors 76

... Οὐχ ἡσυχάζων ἐν πόλει φόβου πλέᾳ.

... do not keep silent in a city full of fear.

Euripides, *Ion*, v. 601

Introduction

Coronavirus: Thanos' dream

If there is a theoretical element of death that both the humanistic classical conception and its more popular version share, it is the tempting (and foolish) idea that death is the great equaliser. Let us brush aside the classical idea that death comes to us all, as if the difference between living and surviving was not relevant, and turn our focus to another perspective that is defended by the followers of the theory of the avenging 'Gaia' or Mother Earth. That theory seems to regard pandemics and catastrophes as Earth's defence mechanisms against those who harm it. It is founded in the problematic of the objective overpopulation of the planet. This is a theory divulged in the *Avengers* movies by Thanos, a character inspired by the *Infinity Gauntlet* saga in the Marvel comics. Thanos is a villain and fervent servant of Death itself. To him, the imminent arrival of pandemics, wars, famine, and climatic catastrophes brought by the increase of the universe's population and the unwavering consumption of natural resources, demands the execution of a plan in which he mistakes randomness with a supposed democratic nature. That is, Thanos understands that eliminating half of the universe's population at random would be fair because it would not take into account who these beings are, whether they are intelligent, rich, powerful or otherwise. But we know that justice and democracy arise from concrete assessments, not from indifference. Otherwise, we would have to agree with Aristotle and judge the lot to be democratic, confusing luck with equal treatment. To Thanos—the etymological coincidence of his name with the Greek deity of death (*Thánatos*) cannot be unnoticed—this apparently just and fair characteristic, that would allow the salvation of the universe from its doom, would be brought about by a click of his fingers, eliminating half of the cosmos's population without any discernible distinction. The population—powerful, rich, poor, and sick alike—would be cut in half.

Now, with the coronavirus in assault mode, Thanos' dream seems to have resurged for those who regard the virus as an immunological agent serving planet Earth. To others the coronavirus just shows that we all are reduced to mere biological living beings due to our fragility to a virus that (as usual) makes no distinctions. Nevertheless, we should not overlook that far from the poetic justice of a metaphorical egalitarian finger snap, this crowned virus—that makes some specialists favour a thorough management of life—actually maximises the mechanisms of power that are beyond biopolitics. That is achieved by the proliferation of 'bioarztchy,' a term we coined in this book's twin, *Beyond Biopolitics: Biopotency, Bioarztchy, Bioemergence*, published in Spain and in Brazil.[1]

To understand this neologism 'bioarztchy,' we need to know that the word for 'doctor' in German (*Arzt*) has its roots in the Greek word for 'chief' (*arkhé*, ἀρχή). It maintains the double sense of chief and doctor, embodied in the ancient Roman figure of the archiarter (ἀρχίατρος), the physician to a monarch. This etymological connection references the doctor's power to dictate the time to live and the time to die. For us, it is revealing that the word for 'doctor' in German refers to chief and not to the specific Greek word for 'medic' (ἰατρός), bringing forth the importance of power rather than medical practice. At stake in bioarztchy is a double process, in which politics becomes medicalised and medicine becomes politicised. This has already been described by authors such as Roberto Esposito in terms of social immunisation, which would have its most visible expression in Nazism. On the subject, Esposito's words are revealing, as they bring medicine and power closer together:

> Why was medicine the profession that, much more than others, granted unconditional adherence to the regime? And why did the regime give doctors such great power over life and death? Why did he seem to trust the doctor with the sovereign's sceptre and even the priest's book? When Gerhard Wagner, the *Führer* of German doctors before Leonardo Conti, said that doctors will go back to being as the doctors of the past, they will go back to being 'priests, the priest doctors,' he did no more than affirm that to them, and only to them, it is ultimately up to the judgment on who will keep life and who will be expelled to death.[2]

---

1. Francis García Collado and Andityas Soares de Moura Matos, *Más Allá de la Biopolítica: Biopotencia, Bioarztquía, Bioemergencia*, (Girona: Documenta Universitaria, 2020) and *Para além da biopolítica*, (São Paulo: sobinfluencia, 2021).
2. Roberto Esposito, *Comunidad, Inmunidad y Biopolítica*, trans. Alicia García Ruiz,

However, the constant exchange of roles between politics and medicine has other characteristics, hitherto not explored by the specialised literature, but which were revealed in the current pandemic. During COVID-19 we have seen, and we continue to see, how the weight of the word of 'priest-doctors' and of politicians, specially the negationist ones who intend to meddle in scientific issues, serve to optimise vital resources for the greater glory of neoliberalism. Thus, both doctors/scientists and politicians affirm the need to defeat the pandemic so that the economy can be normalised. This can be done through classical biopolitical methods, used by doctors and scientists, or necropolitical strategies. The best example of the latter is the government of Bolsonaro. In fact, in Brazil, the population was not only abandoned in the face of the virus, but the government also systematically exposed it to a disinformation campaign and coordinated actions that disseminated COVID-19.[3]

Unlike bioarchy, bioarztchy does not just eliminate or control life, preferring to exploit it to exhaustion or death, so that it translates into profit. Its rationality, inculcated in the mind by neoliberal dogma, is revealed in the notion that income should always be maximised. Foucault's romantic biopolitics was surpassed by the current bioarztchy, which does not primarily intend to mould, control or make living, but simply to ensure that bosses—politicians or doctors/scientists—are automatically obeyed, without criticism or questioning, always keeping active the economic production. In this sense, bioarztchy takes a different step compared to Nazi bioarchy and to the biopolitical analysis that Foucault devoted to liberalism.

The bioarztchy commands, rooted in the pharmacological reason that astutely weaves the new governmentality's networks, using big data, algorithms, georeferenced mobile apps, health insurance plans, and communications. It is, literally, a government of minds that nourishes lives (in the abstract sense) in detriment of existences. But, make no mistake, the bioarztchical power, that leads the medical specialist to play the predominant part of chief, priest, and shaman, whose decisions cannot and must not be ignored, just opens the doors to a biotech

---

(Barcelona: Herder, 2009). Unless otherwise noted, all English translations were done by the translators of this book.
3. In this context, one can consult the extremely important research conducted by the Faculty of Public Health of the University of São Paulo and *Conectas Human Rights*, which demonstrates that the Bolsonaro government implemented an institutional strategy for the propagation of the coronavirus in Brazil. Available at: https://www.conectas.org/wp/wp-content/uploads/2021/01/Boletim_Direitos-na-Pandemia_ed_10.pdf, accessed on December 23, 2021.

fascism that intends to snatch our real and frail *lives* in name of an abstract *Life*. In this new form of government of minds, the best way to serve Life is to become a death general, just as the good old Thanos.

To eliminate legal, singular, personal, and individual lives, i.e. to reduce *bíos* to pure *zoé*, the merely general life, in the name of population conservation, demands us to push aside the old 'herd immunity' motto utilised by virologists and epidemiologists and to embrace the 'herd confinement.' The effectiveness of the bioarztchical slogan is revealed by the constant request to self-isolate and to symptom detection, reducing one's singularity to meek medical objects whose subjectivity and rationality seems preoccupied solely with identification of pathological signs. To achieve that, we are urged to declare our varied symptoms through apps. And, in a permanent state of exception that the governments try to disguise as state of alert, to authorise the total control of each and every one in all aspects of our lives.

Individual life's submission to Life with a capital 'L' or 'authentic life' is not new; it is the most effective platonic medication (*phármakon*)—in its archaic dual meaning of poison and remedy—known by humanity. Its shadow reaches us even today. In reality, Thanos's dream is nothing but an unequalising nightmare that is eager to reclaim total power over a population as much as to further accentuate the imbalance between rich and poor. For such, the political confinement put in motion a sort of post-modern Darwinism that, once we reach the point of reopening stores and public spaces, will allow to survive only the monsters, better put, the big marketplaces, the immense services corporations and chains, ranging from supermarkets to shoe retailers. The intrusion will remain after the virus. Better: It will be a post-viral intrusion, now in the service of immense corporations and platform capitalism.

In this viral threat, Thanos' dream is to create a more efficient form of necropolitics; one that ends up fully submitting the subjects to the power of the markets supported by the eternal genuflection of the State, while simultaneously destroying those lives that seem disposable. This tendency to rule life through death can be exemplified in many ways in our societies, in which refugee camps and slums have become normal. Necropolitics works not only with the direct and concrete murder of people by the States, but mainly through systems of normalisation of racism—understood in a broad sense here—that distribute death, pain, disease and hunger unequally between North and South, whites and blacks, men and women, etc. As pointed out by Foucault, all of that started after World War II with the Beveridge Plan, which indicated that States should be concerned not with preventing the deaths of their citizens, but with their 'health and quality of life.' Today it seems to have shifted to little more than an empty speech based on bad jokes shrouded in the 'human rights' legal spiderwebs.

All of this is not only likely, but it is already underway. Nevertheless, the COVID-19 pandemic is a unique and uncontrollable event, an amalgam of natural and cultural elements whose effects cannot yet be measured. Hence, beyond a possible deepening of our societies' neoliberal necropolitical management, the pandemic opens new possibilities to depose it with the advent of collective, autonomous and collaborative practices. Some of them are able to stand up to the new coronavirus as well as to capitalism, which is trying to instrumentalise it for its own profits. In this sense, the pandemic already serves us well by unmasking what our governments and economies really are: machines built to exploit the lives deemed unworthy of living and to protect those that really count, i.e. those that, more than *are* something, *have something*.

Nothing is yet set in stone, for the potencies and powers are still wrestling with one another. It is up to us to understand the dynamics of our present times and recognise the wagers, strategies, and tactics that have been dealt us, so that effective alternatives to the unsustainable neoliberal and necropolitical capitalism can emerge from these viral times. This book contributes to this endeavour, especially now when philosophy seems useless in the face of our more urgent needs. However, it is this 'uselessness,' this 'excess' characteristic of philosophy, that helps to remind us that human life is more than breathing and existing: It is also, unavoidably, thinking. Considering things from this point of view, we could perhaps go from a *virus as philosophy*—that is, from a totalising and pandemic discourse that dominates all aspects of our existences—to a *philosophy as virus*, to the understanding of philosophy as a foreign body that invades us and leads us to mutate if we want to live. This, perhaps, will be the lesson of the virus.

The virus is something that, being neither alive nor dead, invades an individual or social body to pluck it from normality and challenge its potencies. In this sense, philosophy, this way of thinking that lacks an ulterior fundament—as it is always mutating—can be experienced as a viral agent capable of contributing to the challenge of understanding and acting in a present like ours, when we reach an area of indeterminacy that seems each day anew. Only critical philosophical thinking can go beyond conventional narratives, which perceive the current COVID-19 pandemic as a medical-sanitary and economic issue, and see what it really is: a totalising and unfathomable intrusion into the routine of the planet. It can seed either a new ethics of the common and of care or, on the contrary, a huge biopolitical apparatus at the disposal of governments and markets to increase control and discipline. Faced by this event where the future is suspended and the possibilities of deepening destitution remain open, this book intends to read the pandemic through its inadequacy in relation to the dyads that mark our experience, such as nature and culture, individual and society, life and death, etc. We discuss recent philosophical interpretations dedicated to the pandemic, in order to highlight their insufficiency when confronted with a radically new reality. For us, the central theme, that allows us to understand the pandemic concerns the (de)subjectivation processes it activates. These can range from irrational fear (fundamental to current governmentality) to stages in which individuals become capable of questioning themselves and the political and social environment in which they are shaped. As we will argue in the first chapter, these processes of subjectivation were seldom explored by the philosophers whose thinking addressed the pandemic in 2020.

Finally, no one should forget that the biopolitical decisions taken in the face of this pandemic arose at an international political moment marked by episodes of resistance that range from the democratic movement in Hong Kong to the Yellow Vests in France, including the intensification of anti-fascist struggles in several Latin American countries as well as the demands for self-determination or greater autonomy through referendums in Catalonia, Italy, and Scotland. We were already in uncharted waters where biopolitics was being intensified but also surpassed. The pandemic marked a rupture in this. In fact, it has quashed the many sites of the democratic surpassing of biopolitics. It ushers in new expressions of biotechnological fascism controlled by bioarztchy. These new fascisms that are shouted into existence by people who see in algorithmic control the solution to the fear of death have, in fact, always been a raging fear of living. Against that, what we have is truly modest. It is only philosophy. But more than twenty-seven centuries ago some obscure Greeks discovered that philosophy is an art of living. Not only speech, but practice of the self. Simply life.

1

First Pandemic Philosophy

AGAMBEN, NANCY, ESPOSITO, ŽIŽEK, BUTLER, HAN, PRECIADO, BIFO, BADIOU, COCCIA, AND MBEMBE

The COVID-19 pandemic is an event capable of displacing the structures of thought already in place, and this indicates the need to create new approaches. In this sense, it is interesting to note how philosophers and thinkers of great renown tried to understand the pandemic in its first days. They did this from their own conceptual schemes—some of them developed decades ago—without presenting anything new, as if COVID-19 was just another fact easily insertable in pre-existing models.[1] Although some of those analyses were pertinent and brought important critical elements to the debate, none managed to go beyond the horizons imposed by their own structures, as if reality should surrender to theory. Thus emerged a diffuse perception similar to that supposed answer given by Hegel to a student who questioned him about the incompatibility of his thinking in relation to the real world: 'If my theories do not adapt to the facts, worse for the facts.'

In this sense, before presenting the elements that we consider adequate to comprehend the COVID-19 event, it is necessary to briefly review some of the main philosophical analyses dedicated to it, to underline not only its partial successes, but mainly its limitations, through which we will develop our own analysis. The first theoretical examination devoted to the pandemic, although flawed, is also one of the best. It is the brief set of texts that Giorgio Agamben has written in his column on the Quodlibet website.[2] These were short interventions

---

1. Idea developed in Murilo Duarte Costa Corrêa and Andityas Soares de Moura Costa Matos, 'Viral intrusion,' *Naked Punch*, 31 March 2020, accessed on 7 October 2021. Available at: http://www.nakedpunch.com/articles/308 .
2. These are entitled *L'Invenzione di un'Epidemia* ('The Invention of an Epidemic,' February 26, 2020), *Contagio* ('Contagion,' March 11, 2020), *Chiarimenti* ('Clarifications,' March 17, 2020), *Riflessioni Sulla Peste* ('Reflections on the Plague,' March 27, 2020), *Distanziamento sociale* ('Social Distancing,' April 6, 2020), *Una Domanda* ('A Question,' April 14, 2020), *Fase 2* ('Phase 2,' April 20, 2020), *Nuove*

that required the readers knowledge of some concepts of Agamben's work and, perhaps because of this, they were misrepresented and fiercely criticised by the press in general and by some intellectuals. Agamben has the merit of being one of the first major thinkers to take a public stance on the epidemic and the control measures that emerged from it, thus provoking a series of direct responses and inaugurating the philosophical debate about COVID-19. According to Agamben, the epidemic—today, the pandemic—is an apparatus invented to deepen the context of exception that has been long developing in the Western world. Since COVID-19 would be no more lethal than a common flu—as Agamben thought in the first days of the Italian lockdown—the harsh security and isolation measures demanded by the authorities would not be justified. He argued that it would generate a vicious circle once the limitations to public freedoms imposed by governments were accepted by people due to an unreasonable panic induced by the governments themselves.

Although it later emerged that COVID-19 was significantly more lethal than the flu, what seems to us central in Agamben's argument is the criticism of people who isolate docilely in their homes, giving up all collective values and experiences to protect mere biological life. Thus, the situation of widespread fear caused by the viral state of exception in which we are going through, indicates that human beings no longer believe in anything other than biological existence which must be maintained at all costs. However, there are only Hobbesian tyrannies to be founded in the fear of losing life, never true communities. This is especially so, when human beings are separated by what should unite them, preferring virtual contacts and relationships because of their dread of the other, who is transformed into a potential agent of the plague that must be kept at a distance.

In general terms, Agamben's analysis seems convincing in denouncing the rapid spread of the state of exception and the extreme and hysterical individualisation that people impose on themselves. However, as always happens in his work, Agamben takes the European situation as a general framework applicable to all humanity, failing to notice the

---

Riflessioni ('New Reflections,' April 22, 2020), *Sul Vero e Sul Falso* ('On the True and the False,' April 28, 2020), *La medicina come religione* ('Medicine as Religion,' May 2, 2020), *Biosicurezza e Politica* ('Biosecurity and Politics,' May 11, 2020), *Due Vocabuli Infami* ('Two Infamous Words,' July 10, 2020), *Che Cos'è la Paura?* ('What is Fear?,' July 13, 2020), *Stato di Eccezione e Stato di Emergenza* ('State of Exception and State of Emergency,' July 30, 2020) and other later texts that repeat the arguments of these articles.

concrete differences that exist between the pandemic in Europe and in peripheral countries. In Brazil, for example, the greater problem is not the security measures and the extension of the state of exception—always actively present in the formation of the Brazilian State—but the lack of minimum sanitary conditions for the protection of a large part of the population, who do not even have access to basic medical services or clean water to wash their hands. If fear is the negative affect that makes it possible to deepen the exception in Europe, in Brazil it is certainly selfishness and racism that confirm an authoritarian and unequal historical pattern that is only intensified in the pandemic.

Add to this the unique and scandalous case of Brazil, where the State (represented by the laughable figure of Jair Bolsonaro) recommends its citizens not to isolate but to resume their jobs because the death of a few thousand would be inevitable and the economy cannot be neglected due to a 'little flu.' In this way, if European health measures are criticised by Agamben due to their biopolitical character—which is nothing but the other side of thanatopolitics, as the philosopher rigorously demonstrated in *Homo Sacer: The Sovereign Power and Bare Life*—Brazilian authorities subservient to Bolsonaro cannot be included in this analysis.[3] In fact, they assume a necropolitical character, which is not the same as thanatopolitics. The problem in several areas of the planet is not that caring for life gives way to disciplinary and security techniques that limit individual freedoms. Instead these places show how the State starts to govern through the production of corpses, based on strictly economic differentiations that separate the rich from the poor, and justified by the need to keep the economy afloat.

Agamben's first text was quickly challenged by Jean-Luc Nancy on 27 February, 2020, with the publication of *Eccezione Virale* ('Viral Exception'). In a very brief and extremely critical text, Nancy argues that the exception is viral, since the biological, informational, and cultural flows to which we are exposed would 'pandemise' us all, and governments would be nothing more than 'sad executors' in this general picture. Nancy finishes the article by revealing intimate details of his friendship with Agamben. He indicates that Agamben would be either irresponsible or unrealistic, since in the same way that he inadequately compared COVID-19 to a common flu, he would have advised Nancy not to have a heart transplant, a procedure without which he would now be dead. Beyond this regrettable and meaningless *ad hominem*,

---

3. Giorgio Agamben, *Homo Sacer: Il Potere Sovrano e la Nuda Vita*, (Torino: Einaudi, 1995).

Nancy's text does not make any valid contribution, as saying that we live in a cultural pandemic does not innovate at all. On the other hand, calling governments simply executors of a pandemic-excepting tendency is something more serious. In fact, saying this, Nancy ends up inscribing history in an illusory line of fatality and, with the same gesture, absolving world governments of their pandemic related actions and responsibilities.

In turn, Roberto Esposito responded to Nancy on 28 February, 2020, in the text *Curati a Oltranza* ('Cured Until the End').[4] He indicated that biopolitics—a category that does not belong to Nancy's field of reflection—is today undeniable, showing itself up in every corner of the World. Esposito makes a veiled criticism of Agamben—as is usual in the somewhat oblique relations between them—and says that a few quarantine weeks in the 'South' cannot be compared to the end of democracy, indicating rather the decomposition of public powers. Evidence of this transformation, which for Esposito should not be likened to totalitarianism, is, on one hand, the medicalisation of politics, which is dedicated to the 'care' of the population; and, on the other hand, the politicisation of medicine, which now occupies itself with social control processes that are not their attributions. Although the analysis of the interpenetration of medicine and politics seems valid to us, the uncritical use that Esposito makes of the idea of democracy cannot be overlooked. For Esposito democracy is limited to the 'normal' functioning of public institutions, leaving aside the extremely serious underlying issue—raised by Agamben—related to the subjectification by fear and the deepening of virtual mediations during the pandemic. These are dynamics that certainly do not fit with effectively democratic dimensions.

On the same day that Nancy's text was published, Slavoj Žižek presented his own intervention to the debate entitled 'Coronavirus is '*Kill Bill*'-esque blow to capitalism and could lead to the reinvention of communism', followed by other texts. In the superficial and loud style that guaranteed his fame, Žižek presents a candid thesis that seems to us indefensible: The coronavirus pandemic can bring about a new global communism based on the trust dedicated to people and science.

---

4. Later, Esposito presented his own ideas about the pandemic in an interview in which he talks about his immune thesis, stating that an excess of protection can lead an organism—individual or social—to death. See: Roberto Esposito, *Il Coronavirus Rafforzerà I Sovranisti*. *The Huffington Post*, 22 March 2020, accessed on 7 October 2021. Available at: <https://www.huffingtonpost.it/entry/il-coronavirus-rafforzera-i-sovranisti_it_5e774fccc5b6f5b7c545fa2f>.

Evidently, the idea that capitalism corresponds to a suicidal system that can no longer continue to rule the world is generally correct. However, the bet on a new pandemic derived communism means disregarding the immense mutative and adaptive capacity of capitalism. It may very well turn into a biotechnological fascism that seizes the 'opportunities' opened by the pandemic, by realising, for example, that the individualistic consumerism of those who are locked up in their homes can be maximised. Furthermore, to say that the coronavirus is democratic and that 'we are all in the same boat' is at least surprising coming from a philosopher who calls himself a Marxist. Žižek does not seem to perceive the great inequality in the distribution of pandemic risks between those who isolate themselves and those who are forced to continue working; between those who have their salaries guaranteed and those who do not; in short, between a European professor of philosophy comfortably isolated in his office and a slum-bound Brazilian or Indian that does not even have clean water for his personal hygiene.

More interesting than Žižek's article is the text by Judith Butler, published on 30 March, 2020 on the Verso website, titled 'Capitalism Has Its Limits'. Butler develops the notion of precariousness present in several of her works, stating that the coronavirus in itself does not discriminate against people, but rather people who discriminate amongst themselves due to misogyny, nationalism, racism, xenophobia, and capitalism. Thus, she traces the way social systems construct grievable lives, worthy of care and grief, and ungrievable lives, unworthy of being protected from suffering and death. In doing so, Butler clearly sees that there is nothing democratic about the pandemic, presenting the terrifying example of Donald Trump's attempt to buy US exclusivity over a hypothetical COVID-19 vaccine that would be developed in Germany. Although Butler's text is reasonable and presents fully defensible arguments, it remained useful only for an US reading of the electoral situation in 2020, thus failing to analyse the new precariousness and forms of social control that arise from the coronavirus.

This is certainly not a censure that can be applied to Byung-Chul Han's article *La Emergencia Viral Y El Mundo de Mañana* ('The Viral Emergency and the World of Tomorrow')—published on 21 March, 2020—in which he presents two models to combat the pandemic. The 'European model' makes use of the old concept of sovereignty. Its main strategies to contain COVID-19 are the closing of borders and the isolation of the population. Han deems this model to be ineffective in comparison to what he calls the 'Asian model' which is based on algorithmic techniques capable of 'predicting' where and how viral transmission will take place. In this model, the price of preventing contagion is the citizens' privacy. People must provide the government and various companies with all their data through geolocation applications and other technologies. We will resume the analysis of both models in chapter four, but here we would just like to anticipate some criticisms of Han's article. Essentially, he presumes the existence of pure models—European and Asian—in a world intertwined by hybridisations, differences, and intersections. Well, there are not only two models, nor even pure models. Han's greatest error is to not perceive the emancipatory or authoritarian possibilities that can arise from the crossing and overlapping of bio, thanato, and necropolitical strategies underway both in Europe and in Asia. Furthermore, at the end of his text Han criticises Žižek's absurd position—to whom the pandemic will generate a new communism—and portends the much more predictable exporting of the authoritarian Asian technobiopolitical model to the rest of the World. In fact, Han's article does little to critique that model, appearing at various points to fervently praise it against European ineffectiveness.

In a text of 27 March, 2020, that is both longer and better argued than the others already cited, Paul B. Preciado publishes *Aprendiendo Del Virus* ('Learning From the Virus'). He argues that the ways in which human communities organise their own sovereignties determine their epidemics, intensifying and extending to the entire population the bio and necropolitical managements that had been limited to certain specific people in the past. In this sense, each epidemic creates its perfect and total imaginary body which is opposed by those considered deviants and carriers of viruses, be it the prostitute's body in the various syphilis epidemics, or the homosexual body in the AIDS epidemic in the 1980s. Preciado uses the idea of pharmaco-pornographic regime—a concept he develops in his very interesting book *Testo Junkie*—which determines the control and moulding not only of individual bodies or populations, but of the molecules and hormones that constitute us.[5] He notes that this regime takes the notion of frontier—decisive for Europe—into the body itself, so that the immune control measures previously dedicated to migrants and refugees are now being reproduced within each one of us. Thus, the COVID-19 pandemic delimits a new subjectivity, intensely individualised and semiotic, which mediates all access to

---

5. Paul B. Preciado, *Testo Junkie: Sex, Drugs, and Biopolitics in the Pharmacopornographic Era*, (New York: The Feminist Press at the City University of New York, 2008).

the world through the internet and social networks. Although Preciado's reflections are correct and stimulating, they lack the necessary empathy with the absolute other, that is, with the billions of human beings who are not confined to their homes and have no idea what a social network is, being subjected to classic colonial, industrial, or necropolitical controls. In fact, Preciado's delicious pharmaco-pornography is not meant for everyone, but only for those who can afford it. In this perspective, it is unlikely that the new pharmaco-pornographic apparatuses created in the COVID-19 context will generate libertarian, mutant, or *queer* subjectivities. Instead they are more likely to make even more invisible what Fanon called 'the wretched of the Earth.'[6]

In any case, Preciado's text is important for problematising, albeit indirectly, the issue of subjectivity, a theme that runs through the entire reflection of Franco 'Bifo' Berardi in 'Chronicles of the Psycho-Deflation', published starting 17 March, 2020. Bifo's 'chronicles' are written like diary entries and today they are already in their seventh delivery on the Nero publisher's website. Here we comment only on the first text. In it, Bifo affirmed that the pandemic decisively alters the pace of the capitalist subject, previously obliged to work uninterruptedly and now exposed to a psychodeflation. This can make room for an even more individualistic and competitive capitalism or for a healthy decrease of it in which collective values are in the foreground. But the hypothesis of a 'revolution without subjectivity' presented by Bifo seems to us exaggerated, given that, as we insist, COVID-19 acts very differently in the diverse social strata, of which only a part felt the effects of the workload reduction. Farm and hospital workers, supermarket and pharmacy clerks and precarious workers like food deliverers certainly could not afford to slow down the load, which, on the contrary, increased dramatically as the pandemic spread.

Written in an arrogant tone *ex cathedra*, Alain Badiou's *Sur la Situation Épidémique* ('On the Epidemic Situation') was published on 26 March, 2020. It contrasts well with the works of Preciado and Bifo, which are two of the most interesting of our small sampling. Against all evidence, Badiou states that there is nothing new in the current COVID-19 epidemic, as it is only a reissue of SARS (Severe Acute Respiratory Syndrome). What is new, according to the French philosopher, is the pandemic driven hysteria and irrationalism which is being correctly managed by the Macron government. For that very reason it will not change France's situation at all. Like any bourgeois

---

6. Frantz Fanon, *Les Damnés de la Terre*, (Paris: Maspero, 1961).

State, France is facing the epidemic as if it were a war, including temporary and occasional sacrifices of the capitalist economy to guarantee the future survival and development of the bourgeois themselves. What Badiou seems to forget is that it matters little whether the virus or the epidemic—he hardly uses the word 'pandemic'—existed before; what really matters is the social reaction and the consequences that derive from them, which are unprecedented in recent history. To maintain that the confinement of a third of the planet will in no way change the World's psycho-social dynamics is not only unacceptable, but frankly delusional. Actually, what is at stake, more than the type of virus and the Cartesian analyses that Badiou develops, is the construction of new processes of neoliberal or antagonistic subjectivation, as Preciado and Bifo rightly noted.

The penultimate text in this illustrative selection of pandemic readings comes in the form of a beautiful interview with Emanuele Coccia, published on 26 March, 2020 and entitled *Le Virus est une Force Anarchique de Métamorphose* ('The Virus Is an Anarchic Force of Metamorphosis').[7] Coccia argues that life and death are part of a single process, in the same way that we and viruses are manifestations of an impersonal life that has developed for millions of years on the planet. So, the fear of death that immobilises us today is only a fetish derived from the illusion that we are an individual self. In fact, says Coccia, even our bodies do not belong to us entirely, given that thousands of life forms (like bacteria) and forms of 'infralives' (Thomas Heams' expression), like viruses, live within them. Thus, more than simple bodies, we are bricolages. We are walking zoos that carry and spread life and death in many diverse ways. Although Coccia's reflection takes place from a markedly metaphysical and pantheistic point of view—this is the 'Zeus view' that the Stoics spoke about—we understand that such an approach, though certainly necessary and powerful, is partial. It does not consider a fundamental dimension of life, which is exactly

---

7. We have no intention of exhausting the topic of philosophy of the pandemic, given that each day new contributions emerge. Fine examples of the intense intellectual and artistic production dedicated to the debate about the COVID-19 pandemic can be seen in ed. Brad Evans. 'The Quarantine Files: Thinkers in Self-Isolation,' publication of the *Los Angeles Review of Books* (14 April 2020) that presents brief interventions by Brad Evans, Kehinde Andrews, Lauren Berlant, Wendy Brown, Russell Brand, Jake Chapman, Simon Critchley, Camille Dungy, Cynthia Enloe, Roberto Esposito, Simona Forti, Henry A. Giroux, David Theo Goldberg, Jack Halberstam, Saidiya Hartman, Todd May, Brian Massumi, Chantal Meza, Nicholas Mirzoeff, Adrian Parr, Julian Reid, Eugene Thacker, McKenzie Wark, Eyal Weizman and George Yancy. Available at: https://lareviewofbooks.org/article/quarantine-files-thinkers-self-isolation/ accessed on 7 October 2021.

its individualisation, its interiorisation in a self that suffers, works, gets sick, ages, and dies in the most unequal and undignified ways.

Once again, a certain European thought fails to capture the concrete and flagrant inequalities that the COVID-19 pandemic surfaces, something that only came to the fore in the text of a black philosopher, Achille Mbembe, entitled *Le Droit Universel à la Respiration* ('The Universal Right to Breath') and published on 6 April, 2020. Mbembe demonstrates that the pandemic is just another element of our World crossed by racial and economic inequalities, whose powerful owners are preparing an attack against life itself. In fact, they oppose to the real global problems a fantastical way based in the virtual alternative, in which they believe they can survive the catastrophes that they themselves engender. Faced with the most characteristic and lethal effects of COVID-19, Mbembe reminds us that long before the lungs of the pandemic's victims were inflamed, much of humanity was forced to decrease or lose their breathing capacities. The scarcity of oxygen that will come with the forest's destruction is thus added to the absence of a breathable world, experiences well known to those who keep panting under capital's necropolitical and brutalist machines. It is a pity that Mbembe concludes his acute reflections by invoking the universalist logic of rights, demanding in the end the recognition of a supposed natural right to breathing, independent from the States and applicable to all. It seems that Mbembe does not realise that legal universalism is one of the main apparatuses that determine the divisions and violence of the unequal realities that he criticises. As Simone Weil said in the controversial article *'The Person and the Sacred'*,[8] claiming rights is a sign that the baton is not far away, once every right is a form of mercantilism. This is the extremely low ethical level of the Law, according to Weil.

Finally, it should be noted that at this moment we cannot know what the results of these new pandemic subjectivation processes will be. We can only analyse their lines of force, their tendencies and their contradictions—which none of the thinkers presented managed to do beyond its comfortable theoretical constructs. It is necessary that thought catches up with time in view of the great critical traditions of the past, but without hypostasising them as general theories capable of giving us the key to understanding the present. Most importantly, it is necessary to avoid falling into the temptation to prophecy the future

---

8. Simone Weil, 'La personne et le sacré.' In: Simone Weil, *Écrits de Londres et Dernières Lettres*, (Paris: Gallimard, 1957) 11-44.

based on the present, as if in each moment history does not recreate itself and potentially opens itself to the *novum*. It is this complex philosophical chess between past and future, but centred on the urgency of the COVID-19 event, that we will try to play in the following chapters.

2

Between the Living and the Non-living

What is a virus?

There are many who, from the outset of the pandemic, insisted that we should 'declare war' on the virus. They found it advisable to declare a state of alarm and put the army in charge, with their spiel that we are soldiers who must fight a battle. To avoid this stupid absurdity, there is a simple and objective aspect of our world to consider: The virosphere. Although for many the word 'virus' is synonymous with disease, we should note that 8% of our genome is formed through viral infection.[1] The very status of 'mammal' itself emerged through thousands of years of contact with endoretroviruses.[2] If we could dry-weigh the entire mass of Earth's viruses, we would be faced with the equivalent of millions of blue whales, or about 200 million tons of carbon. In just one millimetre of marine water there are more than 100 million viruses and every second more than 10^{23} virus infections are reproduced on our planet.[3] Based on this, perhaps it would be advisable to reconsider the idea of entrusting State communication to soldiers and police enforcement. Their call for war is not intended to guarantee security; in fact, it reveals their inability to guarantee it. That is why the military are mobilised in the face of the fear of a return to an *an-archic* dimension in which everything is literally possible. It is the fear of biopotency in the broader sense well as of the inevitable bioemergence that leads the forms of undemocratic vertical power to disguise and call 'protection' its ineffectiveness in the political management of chaos that has been going on for decades and is now beginning to implode. As we will see

---

1. José Antonio López, *Virus: Ni Vivos Ni Muertos*, (Córdoba: Guadalmazán, 2019) 121.
2. López, *Virus*, 24.
3. López, *Virus*, 30.

in more detail in chapter six, biopotency indicates an understanding of life that underscores its changing, indeterminate, and impersonal character, but also its collective and creative possibilities. In this sense, biopotency is opposed to biopolitics. In fact, if the latter translates as a policy *about* life, that is, one that dominates life, biopotency is a policy *of* life, i.e. it emerges from life and its processes that may seem tumultuous and dangerous to us. However, it is these processes that continually constitute and deconstitute us. But let us talk now about viruses.

Viruses are intracellular parasites, that is, they have no cells or autonomous metabolism, which is why many scholars do not consider them living beings. However, like other life forms, viruses can reproduce. To move from inactivity to activity—that is, from the dimension of the non-living to the context of the living—viruses need to invade the cells of a living being.[4] This can be it a bacterium, a plant, an animal, or a human. *Stricto sensu*, viruses are neither good nor bad, not only because they are part of our organism, but also because as bacteriophages they help eliminate extremely dangerous bacteria. Even though they can cause certain types of cancer—such as papilloma—they are an important resource in the fight against this disease, as the laboratories of half the world know. However, just as a virus may invade and destroy a bacterium, so too may it kill human tissue. Scientists classify these viruses as 'cytocides'—cell killers, since they 'kill' the cells in which they reproduce themselves. Etymologically, the word 'virus' is identified with 'poison.' We see this in both its Latin and Greek roots. In Latin it comes from *virus*, meaning 'muddy liquid' or 'poison,' and in Greek it comes from *iós* (ἰός) as 'toxin' or 'poison.'[5]

Viruses are tiny particles, between 20 and 300 nanometres, visible only through electronic microscopes and formed by nucleic acids and proteins. They are smaller than cells, which is why viruses can parasitise and reproduce inside them, but they are larger than the largest molecules. Contrary to popular belief, they do not always end up destroying the cells of the host and, consequently, the 'owners' of those cells. On the contrary, viruses have a great capacity for mutation, especially those formed by RNA, such as coronaviruses. These self-select the least destructive strains and lose their destructive characteristics

---

4. The generalised idea that considers viruses to be alive or dead must not disregard this methodological consideration mentioned in Raúl Romero Cabello, *Microbiología Humana y Parasitología: Bases Etiológicas de las Enfermedades Infecciosas y Parasitarias*, (Madrid: Editorial Medical Panamericana, 2018) 126.
5. Romero Cabello, *Microbiología Humana y Parasitología*, 122.

by attenuation.⁶ In this way, from contagion to contagion, viruses mutate to be less aggressive. When a 'new' virus appears, rapid mutations occur. From a broader temporal perspective, it shows that, unlike 'wanting' to destroy the parasitic body, they mutate trying to adapt in a symbiotic way to perpetuate themselves. In this sense, viruses are different from other modes of parasitic life. From contagion, a virus-host coevolution is produced, which favours symbiosis and cohabitation.⁷ This is a necessary survival practice, since viruses can use only their parasitic capacities to exist, as they do not have locomotion organelles and energy generating systems. Therefore, they need to spread from one individual to another through droplets or in the form of aerosol.

As chains of DNA or RNA, viruses are considered the most complex or the simplest beings on the planet, depending on the perspective. That is why, recalling the poetic words of Neil A. Campbell,⁸ viruses are in a semantic fog between life and non-life. In this context, the teleological view typical of Aristotelian metaphysics is evident when it allies itself with John Maynard Smith and his mistake, who speaks of information recorded by nature in living beings.⁹ If we think in terms of the theory of act (*enérgeia*, νέργεια) and potency (*dýnamis*, δύναμις), first developed by Aristotle himself, it is not correct to see viruses as simple information, since they are forms of life (on the other hand, every form of life is also a chain of 'information'). But viruses are much more mutating and indeterminate life forms—and therefore more 'potential,' with no fixed 'actual' form—than we are. Smith's conception repeats the general idea that only what is recorded in the genes can be activated. Thus it forgets the importance of the relationship with the other and with the environment as factors of bioemergence. In fact, as we will discuss in the sixth chapter of this book, bioemergence and biopotency allow us to go beyond biological and semiotic determinisms to which it seems that we are hopelessly bound by the capitalist machinery. That is why it is important to emphasise that, if something opens up in the face of this new pandemic situation, it is either the possibility of falling into the algorithmic control networks and sovereign macrophysical apparatuses of discipline or, let us not forget, the eventual bioemergent and biopotential reframing

---

6. Pakorn Aiewsakun, Aris Katzourakis and Peter Simmonds, 'Prisoners of War: Host Adaptation and its Constraints on Virus Evolution,' *Nature* 17 (May 2019), 321-328.
7. Aiewsakun, Katzourakis and Simmonds, 'Prisoners of War.'
8. Neil Campbell, *Biology*, (California: Benjamin Cummings, 1996) 335.
9. John Maynard Smith, 'The Concept of Information in Biology,' *Philosophy of Science* 67/2 (2000), 177-194.

of the given reality, with which we will be able to mutate (not necessarily like viruses). Therefore, it is fundamental to differentiate the actuality (act) and its positive and negative possibilities (potencies). We will come back to this point later.

Without disregarding the deaths caused by the coronavirus, it must be emphasised that we have known for decades about this type of virus, as well as about other microbiological pandemic threats. And far from consciously facing into this inevitable health crisis, we have instead intensified the political-economic conditions that have created the current global situation. Indeed, the way we face this political-economic crisis will lead us to more authoritarian policies or to more open and democratic societies. Coronaviruses, like all viruses, have particularities that, even though we are seeing something new, are repeated. Undoubtedly, the lack of attention in relation to several specialists' repeated warnings is what now leads us to want to subject the entire world population to a bioarztchical imperative.[10] If the situation had been dealt politically and democratically years ago, we would not now be forced into confinement, in addition to other drastic measures. It is sad to see several epidemiologists and virologists who remain committed to seeking salvation or overcoming the crisis through a purely medical aspect. To think that only medicine can surmount this crisis means not realising that medical decisions also have an ideology.

But what do we know about coronaviruses? Until the arrival of the latest one in 2019, the seventh that affects human beings, we knew a great deal that could have helped us predict and act on the virus in advance. Coronaviruses are 60 to 200 nanometres and have the spherical shape of a solar crown, with glycoprotein antigens on the surface and nucleoproteins on the inside. Its infection radius is centred in the upper airways. This is where they replicate, which explains why the four most typical coronaviruses are the second most prominent cause of the common cold. The clinical condition they cause is catarrhal in appearance. So that before the arrival of this SARS-CoV-2 (Severe Acute Respiratory Syndrome due to Coronavirus 2), one of the most evident symptoms of the infection was the abundant nasal secretion, then called 'liquid cold.' On the other hand, SARS-CoV-2 is characterised by an almost total absence of nasal secretion. During the past year, we have heard of numerous signals attributed to COVID-19 as if they were unpredictable, that is, as if we had the 2.0 version of a new plague

---

10. See, for example, the work by Laurie Garrett, *The Coming Plague: Newly Emerging Diseases in a World Out of Balance*, (New York: Penguin, 1994).

before us. However, all the symptoms mentioned above are common to the *coronaviridae* family to which the new coronavirus belongs. From nasal secretion or its absence, gastroenteritis (or not), through headache and muscle pain, shortness of breath, more or less high fevers (or conditions without fever) as well as the possible development of bronchitis in children or pneumonia in adults which, in the worst cases, can lead to death.

Since 1937 we have evidence of the existence of coronavirus in animals, specifically infectious bronchitis in chickens. But it will not be until the 1960s that they will receive that name, coronavirus, once they were detected in humans. This includes four types of common cold and the first SARS in 2002 and MERS-CoV (Middle East Respiratory Syndrome) in 2012, both with an estimated 20% of lethality. Nevertheless, often the numbers are not used to do rigorous science, but for politics, since they have been telling us the same thing for over 80 years: Coronaviruses cause in more than 80% of cases mild or imperceptible symptoms, such as those related with the common cold.[11] We know that in 15% of the cases, people affected by coronavirus will need to be hospitalised after the upper airway are compromised. It can evolve to pneumonia, which, unfortunately, in 5% of cases, will make the case critical, and in about of 1% of the cases the patient will die. If these numbers now dance with the sound of death, let us note that, as with all viruses from the *coronaviridae* family, the most effective ways to combat COVID-19 (aside from the promises of magic vaccines produced in record time) are: a) Mitigation; b) Existence of a free and effective public health system; and c) Avoidance of zoonotic transmission.

Regarding the first point, it should be noted that since the SARS-CoV eruption in Guangdong in 2002, it has been known that the virus appears in an aggressive way and then gradually becomes less lethal, adapting to the human host that receives it.[12] In the context at the outset of the pandemic, when there were no reliable vaccines that could generate global immunity, the most effective method for eliminating contagion is contagion itself. Of course, we are not suggesting holding contagion parties to mitigate the virus, as was done in the USA a decade ago to produce immunity against the *influenza* A virus (swine flu). We also hope that it is obvious that we are not in agreement

---

11. Romero Cabello, *Microbiología Humana y Parasitología*, 390-394.
12. Ricard Solé, Santiago F. Elena, *Viruses as Complex Adaptive Systems*, (New Jersey: Princeton University Press, 2019) 169.

with irresponsible and criminal ideas like those of Jair Bolsonaro, who intends at all costs to prevent social isolation in Brazil to protect 'the economy.' We only affirm that isolation can bring bigger problems than the solutions it promises. While we cannot do anything differently today, it is important to see that this is due to the total inattention and incompetence of our current political systems. In other words, it is only under the conditions of contemporary capitalism that isolation becomes a solution.

As for the second point, the solution lies in the creation of free public health systems capable of making predictions regarding the pathogenic capacity of coronaviruses and their possible threats. In no way can the systematic dismantling of the public health system serve as an excuse to expose people to a greater bioarztchical subjection based on supposed medical criteria. This is because, as we will see later, bioarztchy determines that the individual, considered in isolation, takes care of himself. Indeed, as a medical fruit of neoliberal reason, which sees in the world only isolated and competing individuals, bioarztchy believes that collective health systems are unnecessary and very costly, and it is up to the individual to medicalise himself and even, in many cases, to self-diagnose himself (*autognomy*).[13] This process generates a subjectivity that disregards the important role of public health, as he will always seek private solutions to his health problems. In reality, the epidemic of privatisation of health systems that we have witnessed for at least three decades fulfils the call and mandate of neoliberal ideology.

The neoliberal measures implemented in recent decades, which caused the disappearance of hospital beds in general, the privatisation of the public health system,[14] the lack of personnel hiring—

---

13. We will refer to this concept in chapter five. To deepen on the subject see: Francis García Collado, 'Biopolítica, Innovación y el Oxímoron de la Democracia Representativa: Autognomía y Nootrópica a las Puertas del Fascismo Biotecnológico,' in ed. Andityas Soares de Moura Costa Matos (ed.), *Ensaios de Desobediência Epistemocrítica: Dimensões Antagonistas na Era das Sujeições Bio-Político-Cibernéticas*, (Belo Horizonte: Initia Via, 2019) 39-72

14. In Spain there are, according to data from 2017, just over 4,400 ICU beds for a population of 48 million inhabitants. In Brazil, if we consider only the capitals of the federated States—with a total population of 49 million inhabitants—there are 22,215 ICU beds, of which only 9,385 belong to the universal public healthcare system (SUS), according to data from the Brazilian Federal Board of Medicine (CFM) collected in 2018 and available at: https://portal.cfm.org.br/images/PDF/leitosdeuticapitais2018.pdf, accessed on 7 October 2021. According to a survey carried out by the Brazilian Association of Intensive Care Medicine (AMIB) in January 2020, Brazil has 45,848 ICU beds in total, 22,844 of them in the public health system and 23,004 in the private health system. See: https://www.epsjv.fiocruz.br/sites/default/files/files/dados_uti_amib(1).pdf, accessed on 7 October 2021.

which does not even occur to cover retired employees—and the absence of necessary equipment of individual protection (PPE), as well as taking into account the population increase, caused the difference between infected health professionals in South Korea to be 4% compared to more than 16% in Spain, or the mortality rate in Italy to be around 11% and 8.6% in Brazil compared to just over 0.5% in Germany.[15] It is evident that, as with deaths caused by the Marburg virus or Ebola, the response of a strong public health system unquestionably reduces lethality. Note, for example, that deaths due to these filoviruses are over 80% in Africa, hitting just 20% in Europe.[16]

In the same vein, one might think that the coronavirus has a special predilection for African Americans in the United States. However, the country's racist and ultra-capitalist private health system is the cause of this effect, in the same way that the more than 13 million inhabitants of Brazil's slums, in which there is not even regular drinking water, constitute one of the many disgraces of a planet surrendered to capital and its mass production of more and more death. Moreover, these are deaths that affect the population every day, irrespective of the coronavirus, without the media paying the slightest attention. In fact, 200,000 people died in the world in 2019 due to the common flu; add to that the deaths caused by arboviruses transmitted by mosquitoes that cause diseases such as dengue fever, zika, and chikungunya infections. These kill millions of impoverished people on the planet. But they do not generate economic interest for pharmaceutical companies.

To consider that the situation we live in could not have been foreseen or that it is not the gateway to a biotechnological fascism that will repeat itself cyclically with each crisis of the capital, means letting ourselves be dragged by the poetics of the hammer and the dance that, in fact, is not more than an oscillation in the face of market demands.[17]

---

15. See: 'Coronavirus: Why in Germany Did the Mortality by Covid-19 Be Lower Than in Other Countries?.' *BBC News*, 31 March 2020. Available at: https://www.bbc.com/mundo/noticias-52111586, accessed on 7 October 2021.
16. López, *Virus*, 87.
17. Allusion to the theory exposed by Tomas Pueyo, 'Coronavirus: The Hammer and the Dance—What the Next 18 Months Can Look Like, If Leaders Buy Us Time.' *Medium*, 19 March 2020. Available at: https://medium.com/@tomaspueyo/coronavirus-the-hammer-and-the-dance-be9337092b56, accessed on 7 October 2021. Pueyo affirms the need, from a 'scientific' point of view, to move from hammer to dance, that is, to put in motion intensively restrictive and algorithmic measures such as those of South Korea or China and then return to normality. However, this theory does not reveal the reason why we are in the current situation and is limited to thinking that after the hard measures of the 'hammer' there will be no further outbreaks. On the

This subject takes us to the third and final point, beside the attenuation and the need for a free and reliable public health system. In this context, it is necessary to stress the need to read books and articles from credible scientific journals that reveal the threat of an imminent pandemic that all governments and scientists are aware of. This threat has nothing to do with the revenge of Gaia, but with our way of life that depletes planetary resources and is related to a double axis: a) Proximity and exposure to animal species with which we did not have much contact and b) The imminent thaw of permafrost.

Regarding the first theme, we must consider its main cause, that is, the destruction of forests and jungles for the expansion of cities and the devastation of many animal species' habitats for monoculture or cattle exploitation, as is done now intensely in Brazil, for example. Of course, the conspiracy theories of insane people like Bolsonaro and Trump should not be considered, but the transparent and scientific alert about the predictable contagion by new viruses that, from now on, will jump from other animal reservoirs to us, as has already happened with the camel in the case of MERS and with the bat in the SARS. As for permafrost, we must start taking care of our home/planet or else beg to a new Zeus in the face of the probable opening of a post-modern Pandora's box, with viruses that the thaw of the poles will release and that have been dormant for centuries in their ghostly category between the living and the non-living.

The desire for asepsis towards the other and the denial of the bioemergent nature of life lead us to wear Gucci or Adidas masks on the streets and to wash our hands so much that, remembering the Nietzschean metaphor about the truth, we will lose the relief of our palms just as the ancient coins lost their minted designs. We will then think that the other, far from being a world, is just hell. And we will conclude that our hands, rather than representing the potentialities of touch and care, are actually tools to protect us from the other, seen as a contaminating enemy.

---

contrary, the knowledge about viruses tells us that the absence of outbreaks will only occur when global immunity exists.

3

Beyond the Opposition of Nature and Culture

Event, Intrusion of Gaia and Anthropocene

The first thing we should consider when thinking about the COVID-19 pandemic is that it constitutes an event. Using Alain Badiou's ideas against himself, we can say that an event is a kind of rupture in the planned and symmetrical development of humanity,[1] a concept that comes close to Walter Benjamin's notion of an effective state of exception exposed in the VIII of his *Theses on the Concept of History*. Events are unexpected outbreaks of time capable of founding new narratives and social experiences, updating the potential times that sleep in the linearity of capitalist 'historical' time. The ideological apparatuses of capitalism serve to continually transform events into facts, that is, in sets of predictable situations, assimilable by the system and that only confirms history's *télos*. Its purpose is given beforehand and 'proven' by certain facts skilfully interpreted. Constantly converting events—unpredictable and capable of opening various times—into simple facts that only confirm the supposed direction of history, the narrative of triumphant capitalism leaves us in a closed present that many authors agree to call extended or long present.[2] However, in each so-called 'historical' capitalist period—'historical' because it is written in the official books carefully maintained by the winners—there are potential times. In the language of Benjamin's *Theses*, these are the narrow doors through which the messiah (or the revolution) can enter at any time.[3] These times are awakened by events that point to alternative

---

1. Alain Badiou, 'L'événement 'Crise',' in ed. Antoine Mercier, *Regard Sur la Crise*, (Paris: Hermann, 2010) 20.
2. A good example of this is: Hans Ulrich Gumbrecht, *Unsere Breite Gegenwart*, (Berlin: Suhrkamp, 2010).
3. Walter Benjamin, 'Über den Begriff der Geschichte,' in Walter Benjamin, *Gesammelte Schriften*, Unter Mitwirkung von Theodor W. Adorno und Gershom Scholen.

possibilities of experiencing reality, which may be worse or better than the current ones, depending on the points of view and the forces at play.

Both the event and the idea of its non-assimilability through the system of facts indicate a dimension that is considered unthinkable. Here lies the old excuse, sung in prose and verse from Parmenides to Hegel: To think the unthinkable—this is the requirement of the event—means to make it thinkable. In this idealistic perspective, what remains of the unthinkable as pure impossibility of thinking survives only in the miserable reality of the immediate experience, proper to the event's unpredictability. Because it is mere experience, such residue is not thinkable, but at most 'livable.' So, it is not the object of official philosophy, but of the confused and chaotic praxis that Minerva's bird will order at the end of the day. However, it is exactly this conservative function that philosophy must deny to think the pandemic of COVID-19 here and now, refusing to be a mere description or justification of everything that is thinkable in the world and that therefore only exists in the long capitalist present.[4]

As we saw in the first chapter, philosophical thinking seems to be lost in the face of the COVID-19 pandemic, going from Badiou's total and unacceptable denial, for whom nothing has changed nor will change in global capitalism, to the adolescent fantasies of Žižek, who sees in the new coronavirus the prophet of a new planetary communism. These attitudes are predictable, inasmuch as the authors do not renounce their old interpretive schemes to try to understand the unfathomable present times. Although, to perceive what is happening is necessarily an exercise that requires a suspension of the traditional categories of analysis, such as the one that separates the living and the non-living and, more importantly, the one that opposes nature and culture.

As already discussed in the previous chapter, virologists and scientists in general have not reached a consensus on what a virus actually is. Depending on the analytic criteria, it can be considered as a primitive type of life since it reproduces and mutates, or a non-living entity because it does not perform metabolism. In addition to the technical issues that arise from this undecidability, it is clear that it also provokes unsettling questions for philosophy, which in its Western version has

---

Herausgegeben von Rolf Tiedemann und Hermann Schweppenhäuser, (Frankfurt-am-Main: Suhrkamp, 1974) 1231.
4. About the bird of Minerva—the owl—which symbolises Hegel's reactionary philosophy onwards and the radical philosophy that opposes it, see: Andityas Soares de Moura Costa Matos, *Filosofia Radical e Utopias da Inapropriabilidade: Uma Aposta An-árquica na Multidão*, (Belo Horizonte: Fino Traço, 2015).

always worked (with few exceptions) with a dyadic cut of the world, so that one part corresponds specularly to the other, as if the inside could explain the outside or the good justify the existence of evil, and so on. Indeed, the philosophers considered the most important in their respective eras have always played with hierarchical dualisms. Let us remember, for example, the role of the dualism soul (*psykhé*, ψῡχή) and body (*sôma*, σῶμα) in Plato, inherited by medieval metaphysics, reinterpreted in the modern times through the Cartesian division between *res cogitans* and *res extensa* and taken up by Hegel and his followers (Marx included, albeit critically) in the form of an abstract 'Spirit' (*Geist*) which, in opposition to nature, indicates the direction and the destiny of human history.

However, what COVID-19 calls into question is exactly the thinkability of reality based on simplistic dual schemes. One of the most influential—although criticised in recent decades—is the one that separates nature and culture. In this view, nature is everything that was not built by human action. The result is that both domains would have their own laws. In this way, nature would be guided by the principle of strict causality. Thus, given a cause, an effect will inevitably occur. For example: If metal A is heated to X degrees, it will expand in N cm^3, with no choice. On the other hand, culture would be based on the principle of freedom (Kant) or imputability (Kelsen). In the human world there are always possibilities of election or creation of artificial imputations, independent of nature. For example: If you kill someone, you could suffer a certain punishment. Now, this rigid division between culture and nature—already criticised by some epistemologists and even by quantum physicists—is useless to think the COVID-19 pandemic. Indeed, let us consider the following question: Is the pandemic derived from, and depends upon, natural or human factors? The query is not just rhetorical, since our actions to prevent and combat the new coronavirus depend directly on the answer given to it.

A first attempt to answer it could focus on the natural character of the virus, which would then appear as an eloquent example of the 'Gaia intrusion.' This expression is due to the Belgian chemist and philosopher of science Isabelle Stengers. She argues that the planet Earth—*Gáia*, in Greek—erupts violently in our lives, showing that all human and social apparatuses are incomparable to the forces of typhoons, earthquakes, tidal waves, and other natural phenomena capable of demonstrating that the planet still owns itself.⁵ Thus, some thinkers see the pandemic as an example of Gaia's intrusive power in our societies, which believe they are immune to the actions of nature and, for this very reason, are increasingly exposed to extinction.

Another interpretation—which is related to the idea of Gaia's intrusion, but cannot be confused with it—sees in the coronavirus a human construct that tragically translates the concept of Anthropocene.⁶ For the authors of this line, like Paul Crutzen, winner of the 1995 Nobel Prize in Chemistry, the Anthropocene corresponds to the moment in which we live. This is a new geological era in which human societies, for the first time in history, cease to be passive elements and act as agents that can change the rhythms of the planet, as if they were environmental forces—almost always negative—responsible for climate change, extinction of living beings, emissions of polluting gases, etc. In this sense, the new coronavirus would be something similar to the greenhouse effect, that is, an apparently natural element, but caused by the actions of human beings, given that the pandemic did not appear naturally, but due to the relationship between humans and other animal species (bats or pangolins, for example). Even more interesting, and regardless of the controversial origin of the new coronavirus, is the idea that it only spreads with the deadly force that we know thanks to the artificial networks created by humans that Laurent de Sutter called 'logistics of capitalism.'⁷ In fact, if we didn't have a world ultraintegrated by

---

5. Isabelle Stengers, *Au Temps des Catastrophes: Résister à la Barbarie qui Vient*, (Paris: La Découverte, 2008).
6. We are not unaware of the criticisms dedicated to this expression, such as those carried out by Donna Haraway, who proposes other more specific terms such as Capitalocene or Plantationocene (Donna Haraway, *Staying with the Trouble*, (Durham: Duke University Press, 2016)). It must be stressed that the Greek term *ántrophos* (ἄνθρωπος), present in the word 'Anthropocene,' alludes to all humanity, without distinctions between men and women, rich and poor, North and South, etc., although some linguists understand that the word in fact designates the human being of the masculine sex. In this hypothesis, it would derive from the Sumerian *an*, *anna* ('lord') which would come from the Akkadian term *annu* ('that'). On the other side, the Greek morpheme θρ would come from the Akkadian *tarru* or *darru*, which means 'bearded.' Thus, the Greek word ἄνθρωπος would literally mean 'that bearded' (Giovanni Semerano, *Le Origini della Cultura Europea, Vol. II: Dizionari Etimologici. Basi Semitiche Delle Lingue Indeuropee. Dizionario Della Lingua Greca*, (Firenze: Leo S. Olschki, 1994), 30). However, although fascinating, this philological discussion matters little in practice, since the Greeks, like us, had specific expressions to indicate 'man' (*anér*, ἀνήρ) and 'woman' (*gyné*, γυνή). So, if someone wants to make a specific complaint from some parts of humanity ('civilised' white men, for example) responsible for the current catastrophic scenario, it is more advisable not to use the general word Anthropocene or use it with the necessary clarifications, as we do here.
7. Laurent de Sutter, 'The Logistics of Pandemic'. The Corona Crisis in Light of the

capitalist commerce, with its airplanes, cars, roads, migrations, cables, networks, and population flows, it would be very difficult for a virus that emerged in China—or anywhere else—to contaminate the whole World at the speed we see today. Thus, more than natural causes, COVID-19 would depend on human actions, as it would be an undesirable by-product of globalisation.

Still indicating the 'cultural' character of the COVID-19 pandemic, we have to consider what Santiago Zabala called 'greatest emergency,' which is the way that genuine crises are not actually treated as emergencies. Indeed, our societies do not take seriously nor face structural problems such as economic inequality, refugee crises, and climate change. These issues are treated as momentary concerns, before fading from view. As such, they are objects of concern without ever needing the major structural changes that would resolve them. In this regard, Zabala recalls that scientists like Tedros Adhanom Ghebreyesus, director-general of the World Health Organisation since 2017, had long warned about the possibility of a pandemic like the current one, without any world government having taken actions to face such predictions.[8] The COVID-19 crisis was there long before human transmission began in late 2019.

But after all, is the COVID-19 pandemic an example of Gaia's intrusion or a human and 'logistical' fruit of the Anthropocene? It seems to us that this question is only relevant, at least at the present time, to outline strategies to combat the pandemic, which is impossible if we believe that the previous 'normality' must be re-established. One of the great effects of the pandemic is the unmistakable demonstration of the suicidal character of capitalism and the strength that nature has when it comes to maximising its negative effects. The natural or human origin of the new coronavirus does not matter, given that the virus's effects are unaware of this division, intensifying itself through structures that are both natural and human. This means that only a political-economic-social system that takes this complexity into account can offer effective solutions to the crisis in which we survive. Such reorientation is impracticable under capitalism because it treats nature as a separate dimension, as pure 'externality' to be controlled or mere raw material.

Law-as-Culture Paradigm,' *Recht als Kultur.* Available at: https://www.recht-als-kultur.de/de/aktuelles/ accessed on 7 October 2021.
8. Santiago Zabala, 'Surviving Change in the Age of Alternative Facts,' *McGill-Queen's University Press*, 15 April 2020. Available at: https://www.mqup.ca/blog/surviving-change-santiago-zabala-guest-blog/ accessed on 7 October 2021.

Thus, the discussion about life or economy that developed fervently on social networks and in the most diverse forums—in view of the calls of part of the population to return to work, so that the economy was not destroyed—does not make sense. To think like this is to think in terms of dyads, of nature (life) or culture (economy) that do not communicate with each other. But the problem to be overcome is neither entirely natural nor entirely human. Only a complete change in our ways of life can guarantee the victory in the struggle against the pandemic. This is because it is not something isolated, but a perfect example of the level of complexity we have reached. Any action that privileges only one side of the problem, natural or cultural, is doomed to fail.

Rather than shouting for the return of normality, it is essential to understand that until now, what we have lived is anything but normal, since it can only generate and maintain a separating system that constantly immolates lives on the altar of the economy. This is the 'normality' of the capitalist system. It is not surprising, therefore, that in order to return to normality, the choice between lives or economics, between nature and culture, is required. Now, it is necessary to deprive the capitalist system and invent forms of *coexistence* in which life does not need to be sacrificed to the economy, in which there is no separation between life and economy, and we are not opposed to the planet.

An important step in this direction, as Isabelle Stengers notes, can take place with an effective approximation (we would say a 'fusion') between, on one hand, philosophy and human/social sciences and, on the other hand, natural and exact sciences. So, one must clarify the other's shadow areas. For example, if it is up to the natural sciences to develop a vaccine for COVID-19, it is for the social sciences to demonstrate the consequences of its monopolisation by just one country, or by those who can afford to pay high prices. In this invitation to a total consideration of a complex phenomenon, there is no moralism, but an urgent demand of the present times. It would be ineffective to immunise only Americans or the rich and leave the rest of the world at the mercy of COVID-19: Since there would be no one to trade or have relations with. Or the virus could mutate and again attack those who were immunised (as it is happened along 2021).[9] Our simplistic

---
9. As can be read on the official health page of the Israeli government, from mid-May to the first week of July 2021, 85% of the cases of contagion have been among vaccinated people. See: https://trialsitenews.com/covid-19-case-data-in-israel-a-troubling-trend/ accessed on 7 October 2021. Israel Ministry of Health data can be downloaded at

example only indicates the obvious element that is inscribed in the new coronavirus: This event is both human and natural. We will only overcome the pandemic crisis by creating political-economic-social systems that are also natural! We must put an end to the Anthropocene as a negative mark of human intrusion on the planet, thus preparing our reconciliation with Gaia. That is also a reconciliation with ourselves.

---

the following link: https://data.gov.il/dataset/covid-19/resource/9b623a64-f7df-4d0c-9f57-09bd99a88880 accessed on 7 October 2021. And is very important to consider the Israeli New Health Ministry statistics of July 22, 2021. According to it, on average, the Pfizer shot is now just 39% effective against COVID-19. Previously, the Pfizer-BioNTech vaccine was well over 95% effective against infection. See: Rory Jones and Dov Lieber. 'Covid-19 Vaccine is Less Effective Against Delta Infections but Still Prevents Serious Illness, Israel Study Suggests.' Available at: https://www.wsj.com/articles/pfizer-covid-19-vaccine-is-less-effective-against-delta-infections-but-still-prevents-serious-illness-israel-study-shows-11627059395 accessed on 7 October 2021.

4

Control of the Pandemic

The European Sovereign Model and the Asian Algorithmic Model

As we saw in Chapter one, the South Korean philosopher Byung-Chul Han published an article in which he analysed how some European and Asian countries face the COVID-19 pandemic, outlining the general lines of these two models. Regardless of the simplistic terms in which Han puts the problem, in this chapter we critically use his 'West versus East' hypothesis to understand how the fight against the coronavirus is done today. According to Han, the European model is based on the old idea of sovereignty. To control the pandemic, the European States close their borders and impose social isolation on their citizens. They create borders within the cities themselves, insofar as no one can walk freely and must remain isolated. In this sense, despite all the changes experienced in the last centuries, the European model would not be quite different from the apparatuses described by Foucault in *Discipline and Punish*.[1] In fact, along with the form of sovereignty that never died, the 'European model' is a kind of transposition and radicalisation of biopolitical techniques that targets the social body directly.

In *Discipline and Punish*, Foucault presents two ways of controlling epidemics—one aimed at leprosy and the other adapted to plague. In *Security, Territory, Population*, he also added smallpox,[2] but here we will limit ourselves to his reflections on the leprosy and plague dualism. In particular, we will consider the differential character (exclusive or inclusive) of the control of these diseases. Regarding leprosy, infected

---

1. Michel Foucault, *Discipline and Punish: The Birth of the Prison*, trans. Alan Sheridan, (New York: Vintage, 1995).
2. Foucault, *Security, Territory, Population: Lectures at the Collège de France (1977-1978)*, ed. Michel Senellart, trans. Graham Burchell, (London: Palgrave MacMillan, 2007).

people were abandoned and expelled from the community, in a clearly thanatopolitical gesture that today can be approximated to the idea of Agamben's *homo sacer*, for whom this figure represents the individual who can be killed with impunity without the commitment of murder. Against the plague, the strategy was different. States opted for biopolitical techniques of individual discipline and population control that remain fully in force today. It is important to read Foucault's own words:

> If it is true that the leper gave rise to rituals of exclusion, which to a certain extent provided the model for and general form of the great Confinement, then the plague gave rise to disciplinary projects. Rather than the massive, binary division between one set of people and another, it called for multiple separations, individualising distributions, an organisation in depth of surveillance and control, an intensification and a ramification of power. The leper was caught up in a practice of rejection, of exile-enclosure; he was left to his doom in a mass among which it was useless to differentiate; those sick of the plague were caught up in a meticulous tactical partitioning in which individual differentiations were the constricting effects of a power that multiplied, articulated and subdivided itself; the great confinement on the one hand; the correct training on the other. The leper and his separation; the plague and its segmentations. The first is marked; the second analysed and distributed. The exile of the leper and the arrest of the plague do not bring with them the same political dream. The first is that of a pure community, the second that of a disciplined society. Two ways of exercising power over men, of controlling their relations, of separating out their dangerous mixtures. The plague-stricken town, traversed throughout with hierarchy, surveillance, observation, writing; the town immobilized by the functioning of an extensive power that bears in a distinct way over all individual bodies—this is the utopia of the perfectly governed city. The plague (envisaged as a possibility at least) is the trial in the course of which one may define ideally the exercise of disciplinary power.[3]

We can say that the current European model incorporated both apparatuses, which, as Foucault recalls, are not incompatible. At the same time that they close their borders and cities, European States demand that their citizens take care, inspect themselves day by day, wash their hands at every moment and keep a close watch on each other. In the next chapter, we propose that this phenomenon can be

---

3. Foucault, *Discipline and Punish*, 198.

understood through the bioarztchical concept of *autognomy*.⁴ This is an apparatus already developed and put into practice in the context of neoliberal 'entrepreneurial' subjectivations. But the leprosy model of abandonment to death also remains operative on European soil (and elsewhere). Many of those infected with COVID-19 have been simply 'forgotten' in their homes, without any medical or funeral assistance because hospitals, health centres, and cemeteries are overcrowded. As we saw most famously in Italy, this even led doctors to have to choose who will live or die, everywhere there were shortages in oxygen and intensive care beds. In this way, an exceptional necropolitics is not exclusive to extremely violent territories, in which death is part of the institutional policy itself, such as Brazil, Colombia, Mexico, and Palestine.

However, according to Han, Europe's sovereign techniques are ineffective to contain the pandemic, especially when compared to what he calls the 'Asian model'—places like Japan, South Korea, China, Hong Kong, Taiwan, and Singapore. In these, he suggests, people would have a more authoritarian mindset and the ideas of 'individual subject,' 'public liberties' and 'privacy' would not occupy much space in habits, social customs, and public debates. This would make possible the use of digital surveillance and the continuous harvesting of big data to guarantee that citizens do not become infected. It is worth quoting a long excerpt of Han's article to understand exactly what we are talking about:

> The entire infrastructure for digital surveillance has now proven to be extremely effective in containing the epidemic. When someone leaves Beijing's station, he is automatically captured by a camera that measures his body temperature. If the temperature is worrying, all people sitting in the same wagon receive a notification on their cell phones. It is no accident that the system knows who was sitting at which location on the train. Social media says they are even using drones to control quarantines. If someone clandestinely breaks the quarantine, a drone flies in his direction and orders him to return home. Maybe it even gives you a ticket and drops it in air, who knows. A situation that for Europeans would be dystopian, but which, apparently, has no resistance in China. [...] In Taiwan, the State simultaneously sends an SMS to everyone to locate people who have had contact with infected people and to inform about the places and buildings where were infected people. Already at a very early stage, Taiwan crossed data to locate possible infected people due to the trips they took. In Korea, anyone who approaches a building

---

4. This subject is developed in chapter five.

where an infected person has been, received a notification through the 'Corona-app.' All the places where infected have been are registered in the application. Data protection and the private sphere are not given much consideration. In all buildings in Korea, surveillance cameras were installed on each floor, in each office and in each store. It is practically impossible to move in public spaces without being filmed by a camera. With the cell phone data and the material filmed by video, it is possible to create the complete movement profile of an infected person. The movements of all those infected are published. Secret love affairs can be revealed. In the offices of the Korean Ministry of Health, there are people called 'trackers' who, day and night, do nothing but watch the video footage to complete the infected's movement profile and locate the people who had contact with them.[5]

At this point in Han's article we are urged to choose between one of the two models, the European or the Asian. It seems crazy to choose the first and renounce the second, which has so far achieved enormous successes in controlling the pandemic. However, it is necessary to see things from a critical and not merely statistical perspective. First of all, the inconsistency of Byung-Chul Han's article is evident, since it is constructed with rather superficial arguments. The 'Europe versus Asia' approach is not realistic. It is not possible to summarise two strategies to combat the pandemic into two monolithic cultural blocks. In fact, Sweden, UK, and Spain certainly do not fight the coronavirus equally. Likewise, China, Japan, and Thailand do not use the very same apparatuses and techniques for viral control. It is an obvious error, already denounced by Edward Said in *Orientalism*. In fact, Han analyses extremely diverse and complex human communities in time and space under the rubric of general and indeterminate concepts such as 'Asia' or the 'East.'[6] Just to take one example from Han's text: He writes that Asia has a pragmatic dimension due to Confucianism, but Confucius is not as meaningful to Japan as he is to China, and even within China there are other traditions that make this reductionist approach problematic.

Han's entire text is impregnated with the rancid spirit of Huntington's 'clash of civilisations.'[7] Like him, Han intends to present a stereotyped

---

5. Han, Byung-Chul, 'La Emergencia Viral Y El Mundo de Mañana,' *El País*, 21 March 2020. Available at: https://elpais.com/ideas/2020-03-21/la-emergencia-viral-y-el-mundo-de-manana-byung-chul-han-el-filosofo-surcoreano-que-piensa-desde-berlin.html accessed on 7 October 2021.
6. Edward W. Said, *Orientalism*, (New York: Pantheon, 1978).
7. Samuel P. Huntington, *The Clash of Civilizations and the Remaking of World*

narrative in which there is a winner ('Asia') and a loser ('Europe'). As we understand, Han's approach is an extremely inadequate way of dealing with problems developed in the immanent and permanent contradictions of the real. In the last lines of the article, Han expresses his fear of the very real threat that the Chinese algorithmic police State will be successfully exported to the whole world after the end of the pandemic,[8] but in practically the entire text the tone of enchantment with the wonders of Asian big data and digital surveillance is constant. Every time Han repeats his mantra that 'Europe is failing in the struggle against COVID-19 pandemic,' he also presents the counterpoint of some 'Eastern' technology. In Asia, he suggests, people would be more obedient, less individualistic and not at all critical of the State. This is why their data can be ceaselessly captured and shared by the government and companies. When reading Han's article, it seems that we have a *Black Mirror* script before us, but without the necessary critical sense that is expected of someone who presents himself as a philosopher.

Another error of Han is to maintain that there is no individualism in 'Asia,' as if individuality was a non-exportable Western commodity, and the Asians were nothing but obedient hardworking bees. Ideas like this can only be sustained with an incessant accumulation of *clichés* that never get to the bottom of the problem, do not echo minor voices and do not see or do not want to perceive the arborescences and the chaotic mutating rhizomes of reality. Instead, it seems that Han prefers to rely on those great categories of orientalism. However, insofar as possible, let us set aside these simplifications and reductions, and turn to its central thesis that the authoritarian, methodical, and non-individualistic culture of 'Asia' would be more efficient than the liberal, hedonistic, and individualistic culture of 'Europe' to overcome the virus. This argument returns us to Agamben's analysis that was introduced in the first chapter. Indeed, Agamben suggests that we ask ourselves: What do we want to save? Is it only biological life that matters in a society

---

Order, (New York: Simon & Schuster, 1996).

8. To convince ourselves of this, it is instructive to read the Council of Europe Data Protection Report from October 2020 entitled *Digital Solutions to Fight COVID-19*. Despite using and abusing human rights rhetoric, it does not hesitate to affirm, as if it were an unquestionable truth, that 'the use of emerging technologies providing distance communication in lieu of human contacts, and algorithms replacing human intervention has simply exploded. Digital technologies used in public places to monitor population, at home, while teleworking or self-diagnosing, or when learning remotely became the new 'normal" (5). Available at: https://rm.coe.int/prems-120820-gbr-2051-digital-solutions-to-fight-covid-19-text-a4-web-/16809fe49c accessed on 7 October 2021.

that belittles subjective freedom (as Han seems to believe is the case of 'Asia') and the possibility of criticism, especially against the State or the market? What does efficiency mean in a culture that, as Han suggests, would have renounced thinking about itself? This seems to suggest that we must submit ourselves critically to the 'European' ineffectiveness instead of renouncing thought, because life is not just about vegetating, eating and excreting, but mainly thinking. Furthermore, note here that Han, predictably, does not dedicate a single line to Africa and Latin America. Apparently, in the clash of civilisations there can only be one central conflict.

In this way, social isolation, as has been done in Europe and shyly in some places in Brazil, is a necessary strategy in an unvaccinated reality. In fact, it controls the *rhythm* of contagion, so as not to collapse the medical-sanitary system. As for the topic of vaccines, it is important to briefly discuss some points here. First, the distribution of the various types of vaccine—which have very different forms of action, effects and effectiveness—is not equal. Although in European countries vaccination is quite advanced, in countries such as Brazil there is a huge lack of vaccines and the process is extremely slowly, especially thanks to Bolsonaro's necropolitics. Thus, it is unlikely that the entire country will be vaccinated, with two doses, by 2023, according to study data from the University of São Paulo (USP).[9] Moreover, according to John McConnell, editor-in-chief of *The Lancet Infectious Diseases*, countries in South Asia such as Pakistan, Bangladesh, and Nepal are unable to pay for vaccines. Furthermore, less than 2% of the entire population of the African continent has already received their doses (data from May 2021). Also according to McConell, the world as a whole will only be vaccinated in 2023.[10] Add to this the possible need for booster or new vaccination of the entire world population, annually, as occurs with the flu vaccine, and we have an extremely complex picture. Apart from it, we must not forget that vaccines are of an experimental nature, as admitted by Marie-Paule Kieny, former WHO director.[11]

---

9. See: http://vacinometro.icmc.usp.br/painel/, access on 7 October 2021.
10. See André Biernath, 'Vacinas Contra COVID-19 Só Chegarão Para Todo Mundo No Fim de 2023 No Ritmo Atual, Calcula Editor-Chefe Da Lancet.' Available at https://g1.globo.com/bemestar/vacina/noticia/2021/05/19/vacinas-contra-covid-19-so-chegarao-para-todo-mundo-no-fim-de-2023-no-ritmo-atual-calcula-editor-chefe-da-lancet.ghtml accessed on 7 October 2021.
11. In an interview with *El País* on December 15, 2020, Marie-Paule Kieny, former WHO director and one of the most respected vaccine experts in the World, admits that scientists do not know the long-term effects of existing vaccines. Kieny says that 'because of the emergency, this will likely be the first vaccine to be authorised

This does not mean, of course, that the potential of the various vaccines should be denied, in a negationist gesture that is extremely harmful to public health. What we think is that polarisation should be left out of critical thinking. Far from adopting a position of denial, we are in agreement with the physician and biologist Peter Gotzsche about the importance of some vaccines.[12] There is no doubt: Vaccines are essential, but we must not abandon ourselves to the uncritical acceptance of experimental drugs approved through emergency measures that have not had long use and testing, unlike what happens with proven vaccines from the 60s such as measles.

In the same way, the salvationist zeal of many people who see in vaccines the redemption of the World and the definitive resolution of the pandemic problem seems to be reprehensible. As we said earlier, the COVID-19 pandemic is a complex social problem, both human and natural, so no magic solution is possible. It is obvious that vaccines derived from serious scientific research are essential to fight the pandemic, but that is not enough. It must be understood that the pandemic we are facing—which for many epidemiologists is just the first of many to come—is the inevitable result of a greedy, individualistic, and suicidal system called neoliberalism.[13] At this point, even with the vaccine issue in mind, we cannot be naive and ignore the multibillion-dollar contracts of companies like Pfizer and AstraZeneca with national governments, so there are powerful financial interests at stake. In the world of the pharmaceutical industry, there is no philanthropy, but business, which is why the salvationist posture must be avoided. Fear keeps us from thinking clearly. In this sense, only a critical view, which considers all these problems, can help us to think of exits and escape routes for the

---

without so much knowledge about its long-term safety.' And she adds: 'We don't know if these vaccines prevent the transmission of the virus in humans,' which seems to us to be quite worrying, especially considering the dogmatists who believe that current vaccines represent the only solution to the pandemic. See: 'As Vacinas Não Vão Deter Milagrosamente a Pandemia. Mas SE Não Aportarmos Nelas, Que Alterntivas Temos?' *El País*, 15 December 2020. Available at: https://brasil.elpais.com/internacional/2020-12-15/as-vacinas-nao-vao-deter-milagrosamente-a-pandemia-mas-se-nao-apostarmos-nelas-que-alternativas-temos.html accessed on 7 October 2021.

12. 'After studying the facts, I have come to the conclusion that the measles vaccine is one of the best inventions in the history of the medicine' (Peter Gotzsche, *Vaccines: Truth, Lies and Controversy*, (New York: Skyhorse, 2021)).

13. For illustrative purposes only, *Gavi—the Vaccine Alliance* lists and explains some of the possible pandemics that could befall the world in the near future: Nipah virus, Ebola, Chikungunya, H5N1 and H7H9 influenza, Yellow Fever, Marburg virus, Lassa Fever, Crimean-Congo Haemorrhagig Fever and Hantavirus. See: GAVI, 'The Next Pandemic'. Available at: https://www.gavi.org/vaccineswork/next-pandemic accessed on 7 October 2021.

crisis. This is a crisis of the system as a whole, something that authors like Han do not seem to notice.

Finally, in addition to any simplistic choice between Asian or European models, an important question arises when it comes to considering the effectiveness in combating the new coronavirus. Asian strategies praised by Byung-Chul Han bet on the summary identification and social segregation of those infected, so that the population is not exposed to contagion and remains 'pure.' Despite the technological apparatuses that inform it, it is, in fact, an ancient technique, like the ones described by Foucault for the control of leprosy. Furthermore, this model is ineffective in the long run, since the new coronavirus is here to stay. Proof of this can be found in the fact that despite having eliminated the internal contagion at a certain moment in 2020, China now worries about new cases of the disease brought by foreigners or Chinese people who return to their country. In a non-immunised population—either by contagion or by vaccines—the coronavirus will be a perpetual threat, a constantly reactivable state of viral exception.

5

The Thanatopolitical and Necropolitical Responses of Bioarztchy

Fear and Governmentality in the Pandemic

'Burials, deserted, and without courtship, competed in a hurry. And there was no safe or general remedy, since what allowed one to breathe the vital air and contemplate the firmament, for others it was a poison that caused death.'[1] This fragment belonging to *De rerum natura*, written in the first century BC by Lucretius, is the final part of the description that the Roman poet dedicated to the plague that ravaged Athens in 430 BC. In addition to the eloquence of the text, which is worth re-reading these days, an issue stands out that bears some similarity to the current pandemic: The conversion of burials into mere disposals made in dehumanised places, deserted, without family members and words of farewell. Lucretius also describes how people avoided visiting the sick and eschewed contact with one another. Although the similarities between the current pandemic and that of the past do not end in these gestures, the differences are also important. Unlike the Athenians of twenty-five centuries ago, we have access to images offered by the media—which illustrate our 'civilised' and 'modern' character—of coffins lined up on ice rinks (as in Madrid's Palacio de Hielo), in churches (as in Italy) or in immense deserted muddy fields, as in Manaus (Brazil).

In this context, the difference between panic and fear is evident. They are crucial, but quite different, passions that help us to understand the role that the media plays in controlling affects and, therefore, in the operation of contemporary governmentality.[2] Taking up an old Stoic

---

1. Lucretius. *De rerum natura/De la naturaleza*. trans. Eduard Valentí Fiol, (Barcelona: Acantilado, 2020) 59.
2. Guattari writes about television and newspapers: 'More than means of communication or transmission of information, they are instruments of power' (Félix

tradition, Spinoza taught that fear is a negative affect—which therefore diminishes potency—and that it can only lead to servitude. According to the Dutch thinker, 'Fear is a sorrow not constant, arising from the idea of something future or past, about the issue of which we sometimes doubt.'[3] This affect is intensely explored by the constituted powers, as it creates passive subjects who need someone to give them security. On the contrary, panic leads to movement. Despite not being a positive affect, panic cannot be controlled by the forces of order and, in this sense, it has an anarchic potential that can be redirected against the authorities.

As Lucretius recounts, some Athenians who felt trapped by panic, threw their deceased relatives on pyres raised by others for their own dead, thus freeing themselves from bodies and illness. Today, the orderly exposure of deaths generated by COVID-19 occurs daily through graphs, statistics, and figures, to which must be added the incessant discussion of specialists, epidemiologists, and virologists. Accompanied by the army, these professionals appear together to generate subjectivations through semiotic codes that arouse passions whose character, far from the ungovernability that panic creates, concern one of the most efficient tools of political control: fear. As Hobbes rightly pointed out: 'Of all Passions, that which enclineth men least to Fed, break the Lawes, is Fear.'[4]

However, according to Santiago Zabala, data and facts do not communicate anything by themselves, as they need several hermeneutical procedures to obtain meaning. In this sense, one of the problems we face today is that such processes are not entrusted to minimally legitimate instances like universities or reliable media. They were captured by the internet and social media sponsored by populist rulers like Bolsonaro, openly contrary to critical thinking when intending to have direct contact with 'the facts.' These generate what Zabala calls *alternative facts* and which others prefer to classify as *fake news* or 'post-truths.'[5] Zabala consistently demonstrates the constant use of these 'alternative facts' by far-right populist politicians like Trump and academics linked to the 'new realism' movement, like Jordan Peterson and Cristina Hoff

---

Guattari, *La Revolución Molecular*, trans. Guillermo de Eugenio Pérez, (Madrid: Errata Naturae, 2017) 401).
3. Benedict de Spinoza, *Ethics Preceded by On The improvement of the Understanding*, ed. James Gutmann, (New York: Hafner Publishing, 1954), 177 (*Ethics*, III, Definitions of the emotions, XIII).
4. Thomas Hobbes, *Leviathan*, (Oxford: Oxford University Press, 1965), ch. 27, 229.
5. Santiago Zabala, *Being at Large: Freedom in the Age of Alternative Facts*, (Montreal/Kingston: McGill-Queen's University Press, 2020).

Sommers. In addition to the apparent denial of 'postmodernism,' they seek to guarantee the construction of a harsh new world order. Against them, Zabala opposes the dimension of an anarchic hermeneutics, a perspective that comes close of our idea of *an-archy*.[6]

Panic is a kind of madness and lack of control embodied in the dreaded notion of a demonised multitude. In this sense, it is a dangerously revolutionary affect which is ungovernable, unpredictable, and extremely powerful. In turn, fear is both the sedative and the music that soothes beasts. The abandonment of our original *an-arkhé* to enter the 'civilised' world offered by the State is largely due to fear. This alone can explain why, in the majority, millions of individuals around the World accepted, between resignation and pride, to be caged 'voluntarily.' The control of fear is one of the most effective biopolitical tools of governmentality that uses biothanatopolitical resources to subjectify the population, thereby making it docile.

In this regard, the idea of governmentality is particularly useful. As is well known, this concept was coined by Michel Foucault, although he never explained it clearly. Perhaps the best definition is the one presented at a 1982 conference in which he summarises his work so far and tries to justify the inflection that took him from modernity to the ancient and medieval world. In this context, Foucault states that he has always been interested in 'truth games,' that is, specific techniques that humans use to understand what they are. Such techniques can be divided into four groups: a) The production techniques (economy); b) The techniques of sign systems (language and representation); c) The techniques of power, which determine the conduct of individuals, subjecting them to certain purposes or domination; and d) The techniques of the self, which allow individuals to carry out operations on their bodies and souls to transform themselves and thus reach certain desirable states. Foucault calls 'governmentality' the encounter between the techniques of domination exercised over others (c) and the techniques of the self (d).[7]

To start, we need to remember that the COVID-19 is more lethal to the elderly and does not pose a major risk to children in general.[8] Thus,

---

6. For the concept of an-archy, see: Matos, *Filosofia Radical e Utopias da Inapropriabilidade*.
7. Michel Foucault, 'Les Techniques de Soi' in Michel Foucault, *Dits et Écrits Vol. II (1976-1988)*, (Paris: Gallimard (Quarto), 2001), 1602-1632.
8. John Ioannidis, a renowned epidemiologist at Stanford University, demonstrated in great detail that COVID-19 is much more lethal for older people, being less lethal for younger people. See: Cathrine Axfors, Despia G. Contopoulos-Ioannidis, John P.

while those who built our health systems and achieved various social victories now die alone in hospital rooms, those who should be able to face in a few years the new forms of uberisation of work are immersed in new processes of microfascist subjectification.[9]

In addition, the pandemic made it possible to reshape working hours from Monday to Sunday, with workers expected to be at companies' disposal 24/7. In fact, what already happened with food delivery workers is being imposed on other labourers, even reaching universities, which long ago supported the banner of criticism and social freedoms. The 'militarisation' of health professionals should also be considered, which, far from having solved some of the protection shortages that they have accumulated for years, ended up imposing full availability schedules on behalf of the 'common good.' Thus, these workers are today losing many important labour victories achieved in decades of struggles. In many States, the necropolitical threat of bioarztchy continues to expose health professionals to 'safe' contagions, as hospitals are not adequately equipped and are not obliged to recycle or dispose of the used masks. At the same time, people who walk their dogs, line up in supermarkets or protest about returning to work, have surgical grade masks for maximum protection.

The progressive dismantling of public health systems, the lack of hiring, the extremely poor protections—often home-made—and the closing of hospitals are not, as some wish, simple negligence. They are economic interventions whose necropolitical imperative is imposed on the lives that are 'left over.' These lives are the same as always: poor, black, unemployed, people who do housework or care (women, most of the time), etc. On the other hand, we have the uberisation of education. The teacher must yield his image; allow it to be recorded; create learning material and commit himself to respond almost immediately students' messages; and spend the day correcting hundreds of papers proposed by strangers who want merely to frame education as the

---

A. Ioannidis, 'Population-Level COVID-19 Mortality Risk for Non-Elderly Individuals Overall and for Non-Elderly Individuals Without Underlying Diseases in Pandemic Epicenters,' *Environmental Research*, 188, September 2020. Available at: https://www.sciencedirect.com/science/article/pii/S0013935120307854?via%3Dihub accessed on 7 October 2021.

9. These, casting invisible chains, compel them to embody the current types of slavery, as noted by Guattari: 'The capitalist solution consists of proposing models that are coupled with the imperatives of standardisation—that dissolve the old territorialities—and at the same time produce an artificial sense of security; [...] In such conditions, the worker will be deterritorialised with regard to production and reterritorialised with regard to relations of production, formalisation and reproduction' (Guattari, *La Revolución Molecular*, 400).

granting of a diploma certificate. But there is still more: it is up to the remote teacher to be responsible for the electricity and the internet connection. The market still requires from him titles, publications and the constant filling of bureaucratic forms to perform his profession.

Furthermore, the new forms of work are widely accepted by young people in confinement, who, instead of being terrified by the current situation, internalise significant categories linked to the ideas of exceptionality and heroism. Thus, positive reinforcements are offered to the youngest, while our octogenarian parents and grandparents are discarded at the ICU entrances, in a clear sovereign necropolitical exercise that decides who should live and who will be left to die. In other words: as the elderly are condemned to a separate sphere by denying them proper medical care, the younger ones are introduced to pre-individual stages of subjectivation that will teach them to be obedient bodies-with-organs and 'heroes' acclaimed by the media. While it is not an equal process across the World, it is remarkably dramatic in places like Catalonia and Brazil, where older people who fought against Francoism (1939-1975) and Brazilian military dictatorship (1964-1988) were hit with more lethality by COVID-19. Thus, we have a great death toll of older people and with them disappear traditions, narratives, habits and processes of subjectification, including some of a resistant character. It is important to emphasise here that neither the doctors who must decide who will live and who will die—as happened in Brazil,[10] for example—nor the young people who are subjectivated as 'heroes' who adapt, for example, to remote education, to masks, to confinement, must be judged from a moral standpoint, as if they were 'guilty.' The fact is that the bioarztchical system works objectively through machinic (de)subjectivation processes—that is, in which there is not exactly a 'will'—that leads people to perform certain behaviours, independently of any ethical-moral evaluation, which does not mean that they do not generate results that are extremely harmful to the critical capacity of society, such as states of apathy, disorganisation, irrational fear, and salvationist or negationist practices.[11]

---

10. See: Agência Pública, 'A Carga Pesada dos Médicos da Linha de Frente: Escolher Quem Morre e Quem Vive,' *Carta Capital*, 22 April 2020. Available at: https://www.cartacapital.com.br/saude/a-carga-pesada-dos-medicos-da-linha-de-frente-escolher-quem-morre-e-quem-vive/ accessed on 7 October 2021

11. About machinic (de)subjectivation, Lazzarato's explanation is quite clear: 'Capitalism knows two modes of production, treatment and exploitation of subjectivity: Social subjection and machinic servitude. Social subjection, by providing us with a subjectivity, by assigning us an identity, a sex, a profession, a nationality, etc., produces and distributes roles and places. It constitutes a significant and representative trap

Let us not forget that the childish behaviour is the result of the adaptive character of children and of the pre-individual relationships that surround them in schools. In there, differently of the democratic values that schools preach, are the lanes on which a constant race is developed for young people to internalise as soon as possible power structures as well as their means of production. That is why children are connected from an early age to new Trojan horses like Google apps or put to work in a 'cooperative' way using computers. These techniques are used not as horizontal and democratic models of interpersonal relationships, but to naturalise the new production relationships that neoliberal technologies require. In times of isolation, these invisible cobwebs—which lead young people to molecularly internalise the new individualising technologies—are opposed to the old-fashioned role of grandparents who, due to the necropolitics, disappear taking with them the spirit of struggle that in the past led them to opposing various daily forms of fascism.

Nowadays, medicalisation and technology go hand in hand, in order to deepen the machinic servitudes to which younger people are more exposed and vulnerable. It is an increasingly accepted subjectivist pair, based on the demand for 'new biopolitical realities' and the imposition of their typical relations of production. Only then those children who now barely go out on the streets will be able to remain seated more and more hours of the day in front of a computer, under the effects of substances such as methylphenidate. The microfascist subjectification process intends to sell this bioarztchical imposition as 'new reality,' so that little by little people get used to it, as if it were a 'second nature.' Beyond that, we are facing the expression of a sovereign power that decides policies of life and death. As Achille Mbembe explains, the

---

from which no one escapes. Social subjection produces an 'individual subject' whose form paradigmatic, in neoliberal capitalism, is that of the 'entrepreneur of oneself.' All functions, all places that subjection distributes, must be assumed as functions and places that we choose and in which we will perform when investing, like any good entrepreneur, the integrality of our life. [...] But this is only one of the modes of action of capitalism on subjectivity. To the production of the individuated subject, there is added a whole other approach. Then, unlike social subjection, it proceeds through desubjectivation, 'machinic servitude.' In machinic servitude, the individual is no longer instituted as a subject (human capital or self-employed). On the contrary, it is considered as a piece, as a gear, as a component of the 'company' agency, of the 'financial system' agency, of the media agency, of the 'Welfare State' agency and its 'collective subjectivation equipment' (school, hospital, museum, theater, television, internet, etc.). The individual 'works' and is subject to agency in the same way as parts of technical machines, organisational procedures, sign systems, etc' (Maurizio Lazzarato,' Sujeição e Servidão no Capitalismo Contemporâneo,' *Cadernos de Subjetividade*, 12 (2010), 168-179, 168)

Foucauldian idea of biopower is linked to the notions of state of exception and state of siege. It is a form of government in which the power invokes the exception, the urgency and the 'fictionalisation' of the enemy.[12] According Mbembe, if in Foucault 'biopower seems to work through the division between people who must live and those who must die [... this kind of] control presupposes the distribution of the human species in groups.'[13] For this reason, when biopolitics or thanatopolitics are not effective in subjectifying their slave machines in the service of production, it is necessary to use necropolitics.

Indeed, the productive criterion of more and more deaths governs our world. Adopting national or international policies that sentence many people to death—as Bolsonaro does without ceasing—cannot be characterised as policy-making with mere 'collateral damage.' It is necropolitics. Abandoning thousands of people in refugee camps to their own luck, regardless of the reason that led them to flee their respective countries is undoubtedly necropolitics. Allowing the economy to condemn whole countries to poverty in which basic foods like bread are elevated to absurd prices due to speculation is necropolitics. It is also necropolitics when States leave a large part of their population to consume low quality food that shortens life or causes diseases. It is necropolitics to deploy batons and bullets against those who throw themselves into the sea in decrepit boats, fleeing death in search of a better future, as happened recently in Greece, Italy, and Spain. It is also necropolitics when countries like the USA, which consider themselves to be major world economic powers, can abandon in pure indigence those who cannot pay for access to health care system. It is necropolitics to have had a president like Trump, who in the 1980s was accused of being a kind of monstrous algae for social ecology,[14] as he pushed thousands of inhabitants of entire New York neighbourhoods into

---

12. Achille Mbembe, *Necropolítica*. trans. Elisabeth F. Archambault, (Barcelona, Melusina, 2011) 21.
13. Mbembe, *Necropolítica*, 21.
14. "More than ever, nature cannot be separated from culture and we need to learn to think 'transversally' of the interactions between ecosystems, mecanosphere and social and individual universes of reference. As much as monstrous and mutant seaweeds invade the waters of Venice, television screens are saturated with a population of images and 'degenerate' statements. Another species of seaweed, this time related to social ecology, consists of that freedom of proliferation that is allowed to men like Donald Trump, who takes over entire neighbourhoods in New York, Atlantic City etc., to 'renew' them, increase their rents and, at the same time, reject tens of thousands of poor families, most of whom condemned to become homeless, the equivalent of dead fish in environmental ecology" (Félix Guattari, *Las Tres Ecologías*, trans. José Vázquez Pérez y Umbelina Larraceleta, (Valencia, Pre-Textos, 2017) 24).

poverty and death, having advised those affected by COVID-19 to inject detergent into the veins to 'heal' cheaply. It is necropolitics to continue to disregard all of this while loudly arguing that Europe is the birthplace of human rights. Today it is nothing more than their tomb.

While necropolitics puts the unproductive of the system under siege, thanatopolitics educates our imagination with ideas related to death to intensify the security apparatuses that are guided by fear. The constant presence of death by COVID-19 in the media is not accidental. Death is the great thanatopolitical tool that allows us to educate *in* and *from* fear.[15] The power that entangles and the type of subjectivity that fear produces facilitates both control and self-control. In fact, it enables the establishment of autognomy, understood as an element that characterises the form of subjectivising domain that we attribute to bioarztchy, i.e. a type of constant self-diagnosis in search of signs and symptoms of disease which is a duty for the citizen who wants to be competitive and not a social burden for the neoliberal State. It is not autonomy, but an uncritical acceptance of self-diagnostics created to merge, once and for all, the management of life with the optimisation of subjects in benefit of the neoliberal productivist model.

We do not mean that death is not an objective or real fact. We are referring instead to the way of approaching it from a superstitious or supposedly scientific bias, integrated in the subjectivation processes that constitute ourselves. Thus, death is one thing, another thing are the processes of subjectivation to which it gives rise and which can be the object of bioarztchical management. For example: A coffin is not simply a wooden box with a corpse inside; it can change its meaning due to the context and the place in which it appears. In thanatopolitical terms, the fact that the coffin appears related to numbers and statistics of death inserts it in a *deterritorialised cartography* as an assigning code. Indeed, the incessant presence of coffins and death count in the media are no longer mere significant codes that provide information. One of its central functions is to subjectify and mobilise those who receive the data. The orderly presence of the idea of death by COVID-19, exposed through numbers repeated constantly in all media, could, at least in theoretical terms, generate panic. But it ends up being controlled by the power of fear, managed by the States and their specialists. It is possible to oppose this order that generates fear and obedience with

---

15. Politics and subjectivation process exercised using death are extremely relevant in the history of humankind. On this subject, see: García Collado, Francis. 'Per a Què Serveix la Mort?' in eds. Pol Capdevila, Francis García Collado, *La Modernitat de la Filosofia*, (Barcelona, La Busca, 2012) 107-121.

the mobilising and dangerous (for the governments, at least) sensation of panic produced during the first moments of isolation. These were the days of alcohol gel and toilet paper shortages. It seemed that everything was going to change very quickly and that the old ways of life were doomed. But almost nothing has changed, as the potentially revolutionary panic has been transformed into manageable and malleable fear.

In the first days of the pandemic in 2020, the mere presence of masks on the faces of the people on the streets was coded through cultural and historical associations. In many places, the masks were understood through their association with even more lethal pandemics like Ebola, or associated with robbery or mass disorder. These interrelations produce concrete changes in the subject, ranging from increased heart rate to pupil dilation and profuse sweating. The mobilising power that a mask or a line to enter the supermarket—full of people with gloves and masks—revealed in 2020 an undeniable subjectification process that, even though it forced certain molar behaviours, also produced molecular changes. For classical psychology, molar conduct refers to components of both trends and motivations that lead a subject to achieve the purposes he wants, while, on the other hand, molecular conduct refers to the physiological elements that integrate an action.[16] Thus, when a subject connects to a computer to telework, molar conduct, his body undergoes a whole series of changes at the molecular level that contribute to its physiological resignification. Another example: The simple act of consulting the cell phone by lowering the head while walking down the street, molar conduct, leads the subject to be in a position of submission, molecular conduct, produced by tilting the head. In this context, the fact that the mask—that once produced fear—became an object of desire for several months in 2020, is related to what Guattari calls microfascist repression.[17]

The difference between the presence or absence of death figures is crucial for producing obedience, fear, and submission to specialist authority, which today is a bioarztchical mixture of doctors and politicians. However, imagine what would happen if each year we were shown the numbers of people killed by the common flu. In this case, fear would also have been present in our lives before each of the

---

16. José Bleger, *Psicología de la Conducta*, (Barcelona: Paidós, 1977).
17. 'These forms of repression are conducted to a molecular state because their own mode of production is obliged to operate this release. Simple massive repression is no longer enough. Capitalism has to build models of desire, and it is essential for its survival that they be internalised by the masses it exploits' (Guattari, *La Revolución Molecular*, 74).

seasonal epidemics, since they take an exceptionally large number of lives, although it is not comparable to the number of deaths from the current pandemic, as some virologists initially thought. In any case, the statistical discussion of death is nothing more than an astute manoeuvre which aims at certain results. It generates a daily *priming*. This is a psychic phenomenon by which exposure to one stimulus influences the response to another subsequent stimulus without conscious intention. Thus, the pandemic priming will make it possible to renew the virus as a tool of government whenever necessary. In fact, the intrusion of COVID-19 develops a relevant and persistent memory because it is linked to a traumatic event—what is known as *flashbulb*—that can be activated efficiently as many times as necessary. Its triggering effects will be related to 'voluntary' isolation, fear of the other and autognomy as lifestyle.

Regarding the pandemic situation, the issue is not limited to the algorithmic or sovereign forms of control mentioned in the previous chapter. It involves aspects that go beyond simple biopolitics. Indeed, biopolitics is not centrally concerned with the individual's self-control through processes of autognomy. Such processes are developed today centred on the dimension of a blind faith in science (or in pseudoscience, whatever) and in specialists. Thus, instead of being subjectivated by discipline or by biopower, the bioarztchical subject ends up being des-ubjectived by the machinic servitudes in which he is inserted to work, to study, and to live. This is why, by the way, the public debate about COVID-19 has been so poor, given that positions must be classified in advance as negationists or believers (in relation to science, vaccines, etc.). There is no room, therefore, for a truly critical view, given that criticism fundamentally involves the possibility of marking the limits and possibilities of thought.

One of the clearest effects of autognomy can be seen in Europe through the results of segregation of medical and health nature imposed from a bioarztchical perspective. The subject agrees to take responsibility for himself by getting one of the COVID-19 vaccines to be able to travel, to enter a bar, to be treated in medical centres, so as not to have to go through weekly PCR screenings (in case of being personal of the health service) or not to be fired from his workplace, among other concessions linked to the self-detection of signs attributable to COVID-19. In fact, this phenomenon can be read as a gradual loss of fundamental rights based on health pretexts, mainly when mortality and lethality figures for the virus, according to recent studies of

29 June, range between 0.09% and 1.63%.[18] In two of his controversial texts—which cannot be dogmatically disregarded, but critically discussed—Giorgio Agamben described this process as the creation of a second-rate citizenship, so that the vaccinated will have a 'green pass' that will allow them to access social services, while others who, for any reason (religious beliefs, scientific doubts, allergies, etc.), do not get vaccinated, will be abandoned. For Agamben, it is a social project through which the vaccine assumes a political-religious dimension whose function is to create discrimination among citizens,[19] in order to facilitate the control of everyone's life in the most minute possible way, such as China already admitted intending to do.[20] In this perspective, we must report the quarantine camps in Australia where SARS-CoV-2 positives are transferred in military trucks, a measure widely applied to control Aborigines. The loss of rights, only two years after the

---

18. According John Ioannidis in a paper published by the official scientific journal of WHO: 'Infection fatality rates ranged from 0.00% to 1.63%, corrected values from 0.00% to 1.54%. Across 51 locations, the median COVID-19 infection fatality rate was 0.27% (corrected 0.23%): the rate was 0.09% in locations with COVID-19 population mortality rates less than the global average (< 118 deaths/million), 0.20% in locations with 118-500 COVID-19 deaths/million people and 0.57% in locations with > 500 COVID-19 deaths/million people. In people younger than 70 years, infection fatality rates ranged from 0.00% to 0.31% with crude and corrected medians of 0.05%' (John P. A. Ioannidis, 'Infection Fatality Rate of COVID-19 Inferred from Seroprevalence Data,' *Bulletin of the World Health Organization*, 99/1, (2021) 19-33. Available at: https://www.ncbi.nlm.nih.gov/pmc/articles/PMC7947934/ accessed on 7 October 2021.

19. In Agamben's words: 'That it is a discrimination based on personal beliefs and not an objective scientific certainty is proved by the fact that in the scientific field the debate is still ongoing on the safety and efficacy of vaccines, which, according to the opinion of doctors and scientists who there is no reason to ignore, they were produced quickly and without adequate testing. Despite this, those who stick to their free and well-founded conviction and refuse to get vaccinated will be excluded from social life. [...] The 'green card' constitutes those who do not have it in bearers of a virtual yellow star. [...] The need to discriminate is as old as society and certainly forms of discrimination were also present in our so-called democratic societies; but that these factual discriminations are sanctioned by law is a barbarism that we cannot accept' (*Cittadini di Seconda Classe*, available at: https://www.quodlibet.it/giorgio-agamben-cittadini-di-seconda-classe, accessed on 7 October 2021).

20. According Agamben: 'This discrimination is a necessary and calculated consequence, but not the main purpose of the introduction of the green card, which is aimed not at excluded citizens, but at the whole population who have it. The purpose that governments pursue through it is, in fact, a meticulous and unconditional control over any movement of citizens, completely analogous to the internal passport that in the Soviet regime everyone had to have in order to move from one city to another. [...] It is significant that China has announced that it will maintain its tracking and control systems even after the end of the pandemic. As it should be evident, the green pass is not about health, but population control [...]' (*Tessera Verde*, available at: https://www.quodlibet.it/giorgio-agamben-tessera-verde accessed on 7 October 2021).

start of the pandemic in December 2019, is spreading throughout the world under a bioarztchical reason that very few critical voices dare to question.

The new processes of (de)subjectification of the bioarztchy are produced and quickly internalised by the subjects under the mantra of the authorities who intone statistical numbers about contagion and deaths. If it is so effective, it is because of the idea of death to which we have been exposed since our births. Nevertheless, to paraphrase Edgar Morin, we must undoubtedly 'copernicise' death.[21] This Copernican twist would help us to understand that the idea we have of death affects the way we live our lives. We would realise that life is being isolated in a purely biological dimension. Since the expert gurus of the economy have ended up relegated to the shade—where they continue to act now, telling doctors what to do to save the economy and, eventually, some lives—it is necessary to start listening to the epidemiologist's *diktat*. The childish search for those who occupy discursive positions of power that are confused with a type of truth should consider what Klarsfeld & Revah write in their fantastic book *Biology of Death*:

> The very idea of proposing a 'message' of social nature based on scientific work should arouse a healthy distrust. It is an opinion expressed in recent years, for example by F. Jacob: 'The theory of evolution explains what we are, but do not say what we should do and why we should do it,' or by P. H. Gouyon: 'On the one hand, I have a moral and, on the other, a biological explanation. And I have no lesson to receive from nature about what I should do.'[22]

And this is nothing innocent. From the infantile image that many have engraved with iron and fire in their brains—that of the fearful child sitting in the doctor's waiting room—we apprehend several semiotic components that make up a factory of bioarztchical governmentality. We could take the field of statements that make up advertising. The regularity of statements about whether something is scientifically proven or at least recommended by nine out of ten doctors, should tell us of the importance of these as discursive anchors. There is also the recurring use of white coats in advertisements, that function as *priming* for the truth-claim of the advert. This leads us, without the need for any kind of enunciation, to behave in a credulous and sometimes obedient

---

21. Edgar Morin, *L'homme et la Mort*, (Paris: Seuil, 1970) 28.
22. André Klarsfeld, Frédéric Revah, *Biologie de la Mort*, (Paris: Odile Jacob, 2000) 241.

way. Other than that, there are real global public relations campaigns sponsored by pharmaceutical companies that, instead of directly targeting their consumers, aim to legislate in favour of their business. It is important to highlight the marketing efforts that, exploiting the usual behaviour thanks to which people do not usually criticise the 'advice' of culturally and socially accepted authorities such as doctors, psychologists and psychiatrists, now presents such professionals as 'cover-boys' and guarantors of the pharmaceuticals. The 'big pharma' performs sinuous changes to impose its 'reality' as if it were the 'real.' It must be stressed, for example, that the public relations departments of the large pharmaceutical companies have strategically changed their names to sell themselves better. Now they are 'knowledge departments.' In addition, pharmaceuticals' advertising spending is now double the amount invested in research; in the US alone, more than $60 billion is spent on drug advertising.[23]

And now we can return to the aforementioned difference between biopolitics and bioarztchy, as indicated above. First of all, it is necessary to clarify that we do not intend to deny the paradigm of biopolitics thought by Foucault and integrated by authors such as Hardt & Negri, Agamben, and Mbembe, but to radicalise it with the notion of bioarztchy, as well as offering new lines of escape through the idea of biopotency, to be studied in the next chapter. Here, it is important to note that one of the main successes of biopolitical theories is rooted in the criticism of the idea of self-control, something that, nowadays, is confused with the notion of the subject's autonomy, a junction that, however, seems to us to be little studied.

Indeed, self-control is not autonomy; on the contrary, the currently dominant neoliberal version of self-control—here called autognomy—eliminates direct contact between external reality and the subject of the unconscious that integrates us. Such an arrangement allows, progressively, to establish self-repression mechanisms through pre-linguistic semiotics that make the subject end up accepting domination while believing himself to be free, which can be observed both in an Uber driver and into a staunch supporter of Bolsonaro. The semiotic mechanisms present at school, at home and in the media with which the forms of power are internalised thus become true invisible educational apparatuses, since they use pre-linguistic semiotics that are internalised in the subjects. This occurs, for example, in schools that

---

[23]. Ben Goldacre, *Bad Pharma: How Drug Companies Mislead Doctors and Harm Patients*, (London: Fourth Estate (Harper Collins), 2012).

claim to be inclusive and enhance the autonomy of students, but do not see problems in installing taps or shelves that children cannot reach without the help of adults. Let's also think of kitchens deliberately designed for women, given their average height. Although linguistically we can correctly maintain that cooking is not a 'woman's thing,' in the pre-linguistic dimension of furniture and space, from which we learn much more than we imagine, the message is diametrically opposite. In this context, any discourse about who has power in the school or in the domestic sphere is partial. All of this contributes to the assumption that things cannot be changed and that anyone who thinks differently can only be qualified as childish, given the supposed inevitability of reality.

As we have already seen, if in biopolitics the subject is anchored in self-control, bioarztchy takes him a step further towards autognomy. Thus, through this new dimension, we intend to make evident the constant confusion between autognomy and autonomy, a theme that, even though it is not foreign to biopolitics studies, does not receive a privileged and specific treatment. The current '(de)subjective subject' created by bioarztchy does not perform only self-control acts, given that its artificial desire for optimisation linked to productivity makes (self)diagnosis one of its main tools. Therefore, we understand that the concept of autognomy—and not simply self-control—is more accurate to characterise this bioarztchical dimension, that is, the internalisation and uncritical acceptance of a (self)diagnosis created to merge life management with the optimisation of subjects for the benefit of the neoliberal productivist model. What in biopolitics was self-control, from the multifaceted prism of bioarztchy becomes autognomy as a juxtaposition of organs—never as a biopotent body—always susceptible to improvement or illness. In this way, the pharmaceutical reason commanded by bioarztchy offers a whole range of improvement apparatuses for neoliberal production, ranging from the classic disciplines, controls and self-controls to autognomy and its demand for optimisation.[24]

---

24. The concept of pharmaceutical reason brings with it a series of universalising, colonising, neoliberal and reductionist assumptions, as taught by Andrew Lakoff: '[...] Neoliberal policies facilitated this because, in the same way that they open the market to foreign products and liquidate the state, they liquidate the forms of hospital care, the training criteria, training institutions, and the public university as the center of knowledge dissemination. [...] This specificity of psychopharmaceuticals is a clumsy invention. The medical model is mechanistic, insufficient in all lights to be able to understand madness... To think, for example, that sadness or melancholy is a problem of neurotransmitters is ridiculous. One gets sad because of things that happen in relation with others, with humans beings' (Andrew Lakoff, *Pharmaceutical Reason*,

At the same time, is evident the social revulsion directed at the free change of oneself that is not directly linked to capitalist production, as seen in the legal persecution of people involved in radical physical-subjective transformative processes such as those narrated by Paul B. Preciado in his *Testo Junkie*. Autognomy relies on biometric counters, such as odometers and caffeine or weight control meters, among many other devices to maintain a 'healthy life.' Furthermore, this neoliberal autognomy requires periodic medical examinations and the most diverse analyses not to measure the quality of life, but to guarantee the individuation of subjects ready for production. From this perspective, as an example, we realise that the poverty that prevents millions of people from having heating in winter is not a problem to bioarztchy. Once sick, these people simply have to get medicated quickly to keep producing.

One of the indisputable successes of bioarztchy in this pandemic is precisely the intense development of assigning semiotics that subject us as obedient machines. To govern and exercise its power, bioarztchy relies more on the specialist's fallacy rather than true scientific knowledge. So, the medical specialist can be a mobilising component of bioarztchy in the form of assigning codes. Let us not forget that from a supposed knowledge it is not possible to automatically derive an ethics or a conduct, as we commented when referring to the words of Klarsfeld & Revah. Today we remain immersed in the priesthoodness of medicine characteristic of bioarztchy, which promises to protect our biological lives at the extremely high price of depriving us of our quality of δέμας (*démas*),[25] that is, living totalities as living beings. The pharmaceutical reason that bioarztchy makes use of, imposes on us the autognomy so that we can connect in any productive environment as bodies-with-organs and not δέμας. In this way, during remote working on the computer, we are body-heads. It is up to us to take care of lighting, avoid shadows, and maintain adequate facial expressions. In this pandemic, the bioarztchy radicalised the symptomatologic care, typical of autognomy, to the dimension of bodies-with-organ that at each new occasion become a specific organ/function. We are now lung-bodies. In fact, we are lungs with arms that serve to cover our mouths when coughing, to which are attached infectious hands. We must wash such hands continuously, according to a scrupulous ritual of ablution almost

---

(New York: Cambridge University Press, 2009), 57 and 65).
25. On the Greek concept of *démas* as a living body, opposite to the simple inert body expressed in the traditional Greek word *sôma*, see: García Collado and Matos, *Más Allá de la Biopolítica*, 41-58.

Vedic in their details. Each of our fingers are suspicious external agents.

Thus, our individuation is given by the processes of subjectification imposed by the new relations of production that continually metamorphose themselves to remain (re)producing for the benefit of capital. To this end, bioarztchy uses more than ever algorithms made by *cookies* and applications that, like filter bubbles,[26] isolate us from reality while feeding our consumerist desires, all at the expense of our potencies as living beings.[27] Against this scenario, we believe that it is necessary to assume the two dimensions to which we dedicate the next chapter: Biopotency and bioemergence.

---

26. On the concept of filter bubble, see: Eli Pariser, *The Filter Bubble: How the New Personalised Web Is Changing What We Read and How We Think*, (London: Penguin, 2011)
27. Francis García Collado, 'Big Data Y Democracia: Educación, Comunicación, Poder Y Gubernamentalidad en la Era de la Razón Farmacéutica' in *Astrolabio: Revista Internacional de Filosofía*, 23 (2019), 114-134.

6

Biopotency and Bioemergence

Mutating to Sur/vive[1]

It is both sad and curious that the medieval cities that were praised for the adage '*Stadtluft macht frei*' ('the air of the city liberates') today are inhospitable places where fear of contagion reigns and where the sad faces of the zombified pedestrians who go shopping tend to express hostility in the slightest possibility of contact with their peers. Far from what was promised by the German saying, cities now show more vehemently than ever the fallacy of dualism between public and private, as the former fades and quickly merges with the latter. There are few who remember these two spheres, and even less those who recognise the idea of common. It seems that most people think that the Amazon belongs to the Brazilian State and that is why Bolsonaro can sell or burn it. Or that sunlight belongs to the Spanish State and therefore taxes on renewable energies are applicable. But nobody should ignore that the protection of life cannot mean a prohibition on living it.

That is why Spinoza's statement, according to which no one knows what a body can do,[2] appears as something absolutely pertinent in the present pandemic, since we must not confuse what a body *can do* with

---

1. The original expression in the Spanish and Portuguese versions of this book is *sobre/viver* (literally: 'above'/ 'to live'), untranslatable into English. Indeed, the preposition *sobre*, derived from the Latin *super*, which means 'above,' indicates in our neologism *sobre/viver* a kind of foundation on which life asserts itself. As we understand it, this foundation is exactly the lack of foundation that makes life rich and mutant, that is, an example of biopotency. Thus, more than *sobreviver* (surviving), we *sobre/vivemos* (*sur/vive*), i. e., we live on something that is unfounded. Thus, we decided to translate the original term *sobre/viver* into English 'sur/vive,' in order to evoke these ideas and not to be confused with the mere notion of survival, which is what bioarztchy wants to impose on us.
2. Spinoza, *Ethics*, III, prop. II, 130-134.

what a body *can endure*. The isolation imposed by COVID-19, among many other uses for power, revealed the machinic processes to which humans are willing to connect when the affect of the fear is activated. To this end, the normalising role of the media in the thanatopolitical service of the power of our governments, which is still being called democratic, has been highlighted as never before. Their daily speeches, which intend to present the naked and raw 'truth,' far from the character of *parrhesía*, demonstrate Foucault's warning on this theme: For *parrhesía* to exist, there must be a risk in speaking, as in the case of the slave who verbally defies his owner, knowing that it can cost his life.³ On the other hand, power has shown that, in fact, *it can*—and always has been able to—speak. However, this is done not because of a parrhesiastic act consistent in frankly speaking (*dire vrai, franc-parler*), but because of its capacity to construct the 'truth.' In the media, power *tells* the truth, but never through parrhesiastic actions, since it works by reproducing the semiotic machines that generate reality, always close to fear. Fear which instead of reminding us that we are structurally facing life in its most authentic form, leads us to internalise it as a spectrum. It is necessary to consider what Deleuze points out in his reading of Spinoza's *Theological-Political Treatise:*

> What is the least harmful political regime or signs, that is, the ones that least invade the potency of thought and cause us to do the least possible amount of stupidity? What are the signs that make man free to all his opportunities? And his final answer is that this most satisfactory regime is democracy.⁴

When we mistakenly think that resistance is related to what a human being can endure or that bioemergence refers only to the idea of a health emergency and not to this bloom made of touches, contacts and mixtures with the environment that is living, we prepare a strange day. A day in which, looking through the windows of a building in a large city, be it London or Barcelona, we will ask ourselves: 'Why don't I take the streets? Where does this feeling of longing and anxiety come from? What is happening to me?.' This is called desire. We are being rebuilt so that we feel sick thanks to the simple desire to go for a walk. According to Guattari: 'Every time, faced with a desire, we ask

---

3. Regarding *parrhesía* in Foucault's thought, see: Michel Foucault, *The Government of Self and Others: Lectures at the Collège de France (1982-1983)*, ed. Arnold I. Davidson, trans. Graham Burchell, (New York: Palgrave Macmillan, 2010).
4. Gilles Deleuze, *En Medio de Spinoza*, trans. Equipo Cactus, (Buenos Aires: Cactus, 2017) 198.

ourselves "what does this mean?," do not be confused: what happens is that a formation of power is taking place and it asks us for accounts.'[5] Well, are we going to stay connected at home, like batteries that feed the capital, chained to computers that subject us to remote work, full of resignation and fear of taking the streets? The issue here does not concern the supposed fair, necessary, or emergency character of the lockdown, which would make people more docile. After all, in several European countries people protested against lockdown (in Brazil, which in recent times has become a surreal example of almost everything, people protested against the lack of confinement). Furthermore, lockdown, as a new form of bioarztchical power, also generates new biopotent resistances, such as many children and adolescents have experienced when they simply disregarded the orders of the authorities and took to the streets. As Foucault taught, all power necessarily involves resistance. In this way, what interests us to discuss here is the transforming, mutating, and indeterminate potencies of bodies, which bioarztchy at all times intends to block and canalise for its own objectives. In fact, what can a δέμας (*démas*) do? What can a living being (as living being) do?

We can remain thinking that all the apparatuses we connect to serve to provide information or even tell us the truth, like who, in the middle of a desert, fall into the trap of his brain, believing he hear the voice of a god, but in reality this one is having an auditory illusion thanks to the heat. There are signs that, as Adam Phillips says, 'we are inevitably faithful to the dead body that grows within us.'[6] The distance that separates us from autonomy is of the same nature of the power that compels us, for example, to live in family. The proto-italic term *famelos (servant) is a clear etymological evidence that the word 'family' alludes to a group of slaves who need each other to survive and among whose aspirations the pleasure of living life does not seem to be.[7] Pandemic isolation is similar to this situation, but not because of what we experience today. Except for the comings and goings to work before confinement, everything might have already been like this before. Between the acceptance of the dead body that grows within us and the biopotential and bioemergent response to what a body can do, it is the

---

5. Guattari, *La Revolución Molecular*, 219.
6. Adam Phillips, *Monogamia*, trans. Daniel Najmías, (Barcelona: Anagrama, 1998), 13.
7. For example, in Catalan *fam* means to be hungry and in Portuguese and Castilian *famélico* is linked to the expression 'estar morto de fome,' literally 'being dead from hunger,' namely 'being starving.'

openness to life. So, it is necessary not only to verbalise the answer, but to let ourselves be carried away by the parrhesiastic saying that is made of actions, opening the front door and, considering the two symbiotic aspects of a statement,[8] exercising a performative act full of meaning, as if we were to cross a Rubicon. And not to rebuild any 'normality' and return to work for the capital, but to assume the indeterminacy of reality and create other possible worlds. If the pandemic taught us that the life we lived was still not the worst one possible and that it could become even more dead and meaningless, it is up to us to invert that lesson. In this way, we need to understand that a life of potency is one in which we not only survive, but sur/vive, that is, we live it founded on an absence of foundation that can free us from the sad affect of fear and open the doors to a mutant contagion with ourselves.

Here it is necessary to devote a few words to the notion of biopotency. With this idea, we intend to offer an original contribution to the debates about biopolitics that have been developing for decades in fields as diverse as bioethics, political philosophy, neuroscience and ontology. Today, this debate seems to have reached one of its limits in the context of the COVID-19 pandemic. In the twenty-first century, our societies can no longer be analysed simply as disciplinary, control, consumer, or spectacle societies. Indeed, neoliberal capitalism has fused these variants into an undifferentiated amalgam that denies any narrative or experience that does not submit to its quantitative and self-controlling determinations. As we saw, such determinations are translated into a bioarztchy in which the medical-pharmaceutical power is combined with technologies and apparatuses of (de)subjectivation aimed at creating a 'productive' and entrepreneurial, stupid, and authoritarian world.

In this context, we understand that only a biopotent thought can deactivate the bio, thanato, and necropolitical mechanisms used by capital to reproduce itself. In fact, neoliberal biopolitical power can only operate from a close relationship with the general matrix of economic logic, according to which goods are scarce. Now, if life is the most important of goods, nothing prevents it from entering the equations of the famous 'science of scarce goods.' It is as if vitality is a rare type of resource or property that causes human beings to compete mortally,

---

8. 'In each statement there are two fundamental aspects, symbiotic but very different: a) What is said, the semantic content expressed in the statement thanks to certain phonetic, lexical, syntactic characters; b) The fact that one speaks, that the word is taken breaking the silence, the act of enunciating as such, the speaker's exposure in front of others' (Paolo Virno, *Cuando el Verbo se Hace Carne*, trans. Eduardo Sadier, (Madrid: Cactus, 2005) 61).

so that the lives of some depend on the death of others. Foucault recognised in this apparatus, conceptualising it as 'State racism,' a social management machine whereby the maximisation of the life of a certain community depends on the extermination of other lives understood as competing parasites.[9] It is, in fact, the basic principle of neoliberalism, which, by presupposing universal competition, determines that some can only live while others die, or rather, some live at the expense of the death of others. Bioarztchy deepens this logic, leading people to transform themselves to become healthy servants of capital, always aware of the need for physical-mental optimisations, so that they are always 'happy,' 'young,' and 'beautiful' (there are countless legal and illegal drugs to do so). If they are not recycled according to the dominant model of 'Life' (with capitals), they are left to die outside society. Thus, it is clear that death is essential for the economy of Life, at least as long as it is viewed biopolitically, that is, as a scarce resource always disputed by the growing human masses.

Here is one of the clear limitations of neoliberal biopolitical thought, which by understanding life as a 'thing' or an 'entity,' makes possible its immediate conversion into a commodity, into a scarce good to be appropriated, even violently. To escape this fatal bipolar machine, it is necessary to think about life from a different point of view, which does not see it as a thing, but as a process. Life *is* not something, but it *is always being* something, it is building, developing, multiplying, and losing itself. Against the idea of life as a scarce good for which humans struggle, one can oppose the image of an infinite reservoir of life, an ever-increasing and changing impersonal potency of vitality that denies competition and favours hybridisation, cooperation, and miscegenation. Against the conception of a limited block of vitality that not everyone can access because that way it would be exhausted, we oppose the immanent potency of life that continually arises from itself. The name of this thought (and this practice) still unthought by our societies is biopotency. We must address it if we do not want to head towards an unprecedented (thanato)(necro)(bio)political catastrophe.

The potency of life becomes singular in the body. Only through it can we think of a biopotency that faces life not as an abstract universal concept, 'protected' by bioarztchical governments and markets. On the contrary, the body offers an immanent field in which life is constantly

---

9. Michel Foucault, *Society Must be Defended: Lectures at the Collège de France (1975-1976)*, eds. Mauro Bertani and Alessandro Fontana, trans. David Macey, (London: Penguin, 2003) 254 *et seq.*

singularised in its multiple variations in humans, animals, and plants. In this way, the biopotency is opposed to the biopolitical notion according to which all politics of life are translatable into thanatopolitics. In this wrong idea, life is outside of itself. It was transformed into object of managements that take death as a reference to decide on policies of life, as is the case in the pandemic. In addition to the massacres carried out in the name of Life that many may consider exceptional, the 'normal' language of this type of approach has been familiar to us for decades: risk, insurance, medical check-up, examination, control, among many other ways to guide life from a thanatological perspective. When we abandon the traditional concept of biopolitics and assume the idea of biopotency, we cannot ignore that this change is only possible because it is related to the opening of singular and concrete bodies, not to the mere abstract and mechanical Life protected by bioarztchy.

Hardt & Negri realise that what is really at stake in the idea of contagion is the notion of mixture. In this sense, contagion needs to be understood less as a medical term and more as an ontological category. Obviously, it is a very different ontology from the dual and conservative one that always separates and hierarchises reality, which we talked about in chapter three. In contrast, contagion is interpreted by us as a biopotent dimension that opposes purity and uniqueness, privileging mixture, miscegenation, excess, and hybridisation. Mixture poses the challenge to never be one. Blending, disintegration, and assimilation with the world are the key. Only by mixing ourselves with the world we can actually live. We must see in the COVID-19 pandemic a kind of mixture. The mixture—it does not matter if we like it or not—is in all of us. It is impossible to keep ourselves pure and immaculate. This disturbing condition shows us that we are all vulnerable, even though, of course, pandemic risks are unevenly distributed. However, the pandemic proves that, in a way, most of humanity is now involved in a process that Achille Mbembe called 'becoming black'. In the introduction of his book *Critique of Black Reason*, entitled 'The Becoming Black of the World,' Mbembe does not treat 'being black' as a simply racial or historical category, but mainly as a mark of abandonment, lack of care, oppression, and exploitation that, having once imposed on enslaved black bodies, it is now globalised.[10]

---

10. It is important to read Mbembe's words to avoid any misunderstandings: 'First, the systematic risks experienced specifically by Black slaves during early capitalism have now become the norm for, or at least the lot of, all of subaltern humanity. The emergence of new imperial practices is then tied to the tendency to universalise the Black condition. Such practices borrow as much from the slaving logic of capture and

The skin is the privileged vehicle of contagion, because everything touched by a human may have become a nest for COVID-19. Thus, our societies deepen the neoliberal tendency towards dematerialisation and mediation, reserving to the poor the tasks that require continuous contact, this ever-present risk of infection. Indeed, in the pandemic we reserve the same deadly identification with the virus for the poor (especially poor women), even though we demand that they continue cleaning our houses and streets, delivering our purchases and cooking our food.[11] Such a situation will continue after the pandemic and will become the rule. In a truly short time, contact and contagion will become synonymous and will be equally despised and feared as 'things of the poor.' When that happens, we can be sure that we have reached the end.

Life is fundamentally a transindividual and transpersonal condition that has no obligation to human psychic-subjective systems that insist on reducing it to a 'self.' Unlike the entities that contain it momentarily, life is always surplus, it is always an excessive gift that circulates and demands the continuity of circulation, as Georges Bataille knew well.[12] It is then necessary to reformulate the famous sentence of the physiologist Xavier Bichat, for whom 'life is the set of functions that resists death.'[13] On the contrary, it is death that propels life, in the

---

predation as from the colonial logic of occupation and extraction, as well as from the civil wars and raiding of earlier epochs. Wars of occupation and counterinsurgency aim not only to track and eliminate the enemy but also to create a partition in time and an atomisation of space. In the future, part of the task of empire will consist in transforming the real into fiction, and fiction into the real. The mobilisation of airpower and the destruction of infrastructure, the strikes and wounds caused by military action, are now combined with the mass mobilisation of images, a key part of the deployment of a violence that seeks purity. [...] Across early capitalism, the term 'Black' referred only to the condition imposed on peoples of African origin (different forms of depredation, dispossession of all power of self-determination, and, most of all, dispossession of the future and of time, the two matrices of the possible). Now, for the first time in human history, the term 'Black' has been generalised. This new fungibility, this solubility, institutionalised as a new norm of existence and expanded to the entire planet, is what I call the Becoming Black of the world' (Achille Mbembe, *Critique of Black Reason*, (Durham: Duke University Press, 2017) 4-6).

11. Following the intuition of Hardt & Negri, the word 'poor' does not refer exclusively to those deprived of economic resources, but to all those who, members of the multitude, are put to work for the Empire and thus lose control of their lives. See: Michael Hardt, Antonio Negri, *Commonwealth*, (Cambridge: Harvard University Press, 2009) 39-55.

12. Georges Bataille, 'The Notion of Expenditure' in Georges Bataille, *The Bataille Reader*, eds. Fred Botting and Scott Wilson, (Oxford: Blackwell, 1997) 167-181.

13. Xavier Bichat, *Recherches Physiologiques Sur la Vie et Sur la Mort*, (Genève/Paris/Bruxelles: Alliance Culturelle du Livre, 1962) 43.

same way that COVID-19, in its bioemergent dimension, challenges capitalist survival and points to a gap that Foucault was able to intuit in the last text he published before his death—an article dedicated to his former master Georges Canguilhem. According Canguilhem, health has to do not with the self-preservation of a body, but with its capacity for self-transformation. Foucault starts from this idea to find the truth of life in error. In fact, if we think about life in this radical way, being alive is being capable of making mistakes. Only through errors does life move forward and continually emerge from itself, so that all knowledge that explores life should be redirected towards errors and not supposed truths. In this sense, life is, literally, *err*, wandering. After all, what is knowledge about life if not a long and discontinuous series of errors accompanied by their corrections?[14]

Here the idea of bioemergence comes up, with all its chaotic and creative charge. Quite obviously, it is a neologism based on the junction of the words '*bíos*' and 'emergence.' In it, the notion of 'emergence' is linked to the verb 'to emerge' as conceived in biology by the anthropologist Terrence Deacon. It is an emergency that refers not to an urgency,[15] but to arising, to emerging.[16] In this perspective,

---

14. 'At the center of these problems one finds that of error. For, at the most basic level of life, the processes of coding and decoding give way to a chance occurrence that, before becoming a disease, a deficiency, or a monstrosity, is something like a disturbance in the informative system, something like a 'mistake.' In this sense, life—and this is its radical feature—is that which is capable of error. And perhaps it is this datum or rather this contingency which must be asked to account for the fact that the question of anomaly permeates the whole of biology. And it must also be asked to account for the mutations and evolutive processes to which they lead. Further, it must be questioned in regard to that singular but hereditary error which explains the fact that, with man, life has led to a living being that is never completely in the right place, that is destined to 'err' and to be 'wrong.' And if one grants that the concept is the reply that life itself has given to that chance process, one must agree that error is the root of what produces human thought and its history. The opposition of the true and the false, the values that are attributed to the one and the other, the power effects that different societies and different institutions link to that division—all this may be nothing but the most belated response to that possibility of error inherent in life. If the history of the sciences is discontinuous—that is, if it can be analysed only as a series of 'corrections,' as a new distribution that never sets free, finally and forever, the terminal moment of truth—the reason, again, is that 'error' constitutes not a neglect or a delay of the promised fulfillment but the dimension peculiar to the life of human beings and indispensable to the duration [*temps*] of the species' (Michel Foucault, 'Life: Experience and Science' in Michel Foucault, *Aesthetics, Method, and Epistemology: Essential Works of Foucault (1954-1984), Vol. Two*. Ed. James D. Faubion, trans. Robert Hurley, (New York: The New Press, 1998) 476).
15. About the idea of emergency as urgency in general, it is worth reading the chapter "Emergency and Biodiversity" in Zabala, *Being at Large*, 145-149.
16. Terrence W. Deacon, *Incomplete Nature: How Mind Emerged from Matter*, (New York: Norton, 2013) 143-181.

as Esposito explains when referring to Merleau-Ponty's work, the concept of emergence is not related to the notion of constitutive power, which always requires a presupposed subject prior to formative processes, but rather to instituting praxis. This indicates something that emerges from something else without being determined by it, but, on the contrary, transforming it into a virtually infinite process.[17]

In *Difference and Repetition*, Gilles Deleuze criticises the traditional process of Western philosophy that consists in the construction of abstract universal concepts (for example, 'the' man) based on particulars (an English man, a socialist man, a man named John) that are just reflexes of the emptiness of the universal, which is never present anywhere, neither as an act nor as a potency. It is precisely this process that bioarztchy uses to control Life in general and condemn the smaller and concrete lives. Thus, instead of using the notion of particular, which is nothing more than a phantasmatic derivation of the idea of universal, Deleuze proposes the concept of *singularity*, which is radically concerned with the uniqueness of each being.

Without being able to go deeper into Deleuze's complex argument, we understand that the main question of his ontology is: How does something new appear in the world? To do so, he makes use of two dyads that do not mix—possible/real and virtual/actual. The possible depends on the real, since what is possible derives from the really existing. In this sense, it is not possible for an orange to be born from an apple tree. But if the world were really like that, how would the novelty—or, in our words, the (bio)emergence of the new—emerge in it? How, for example, did the human being come from eukaryotic cells? How would consciousness have emerged from pure inorganic and amorphous matter?

To solve this difficulty, Deleuze and Guattari present in their last book, *What is Philosophy?*, the virtual/actual dyad, explaining that the virtual—or potential, in our terms—does not depend on the actual, it does not resemble it and cannot be predicted from it. Indeed, the virtual extrapolates the actual. With the virtual come the multiplicities. Multiplicities are differential repetitions of singularities, which can be thought as constants (as science does) or as pure variations (as philosophy does). Thus, philosophy is built through self-referent concepts. It deals with the chaos that emerges from the real, something that science cannot and does not intend to do, as it establishes limits between the

---

17. Roberto Esposito, *Istituzione*, (Bologna: Il Mulino, 2021) 55-56.

variables and works with constants, that is, a relatively acceptable type of 'universal.'

We are not, therefore, the result of a card marking process between potency and act; we are touch, gesture, bodies, signifiers, skeins, affections, immersions, contagion and caress, but also wound, blow, impact, shock. Something like the potentiation of a potency, a potency that is autonomous in relation to the act, which is openness and continuous emergence *of* itself and *in* itself: World. In the *bíos* dimension, thinking about potency without considering emergence and chance prevents us from recognising an important biological principle described by Steven Rose, for whom the unity of organisms is not something structurally given once and for all. This means that living systems are open.[18]

Life and its processes largely arise from unforeseen, uncontrollable and irreducible emergences, as only in this way can the new emerge. If someone can become a flautist, it does not happen because there have always been flautists. The first flautist did not have in front of him a 'knowing how' to be a flautist.[19] It was bioemergence, chance—and not the overestimated causality—contact, experimentation and game that led a certain primitive human to introduce, perhaps bored, a hollow bone in his mouth and blow, thus creating 'flautism.' There is no potency in general, but potencies of emergence and chance.

Therefore, every idea of potency must be reinterpreted as bioemergence. We are not something fixed or a jumble of potencies and acts, but an ever-emerging *bíos* that maintains the fascination of biochemist Jacques Monod's question, who wonders how it was possible that purposeful systems, such as humans, have emerged from a universe without goals. The answer lies in the notion of bioemergence. We write even though we do not have specific genes for this, and if it occurs an eventual resurgence of humanity after some probable catastrophic extinction, there is no guarantee that writing will develop again.[20] There

---

18. 'The unity of an organism is a process unity, not a structural one... This means that living systems are open... Every living creature is in constant flux, always at the same time both *being* and *becoming*' (Steven Rose, 'Levels of Explanation in Human Behaviour: The Poverty of Evolutionary Psychology,' in eds. David L. Hull, Marc H. V. van Regenmortel, *Promises and Limits of Reductionism in the Biomedical Sciences*, (West Sussex: John Wiley and Sons, 2002) 290).
19. This example of the flautist is inspired by Aristotle, who uses it to discuss in his own way the relationship between act and potency. See: Aristotle, *Metaphysics*, 1049b30-1050a5.
20. Maryanne Wolf, *Cómo Aprendemos a Leer*, trans. Martín Rodríguez-Courel, (Barcelona: Ediciones B, 2008) 232.

is no inner magic that projects itself to the outside. We *are* because *there is* flow and chance.

The 'great health' envisioned by Nietzsche is not in the normalisations or homologations required by the neoliberal bioarztchy, but in the errors that continually emerge and (de)constitute us. From an ethical point of view, we propose to call such errors contagion, which is now our inevitable epochal condition. We can think of contagion as a dimension of the emergency alluded by Cornelius Castoriadis in the context of instituting practices. It is a process that does not presuppose a previous subject and is not controlled by anyone.[21] Although the erratic and contagious emergence of life is not absolute, it does not simply derive, like the legal rules, from a general framework. It shows itself as a *novum* that *alters the origin* in the same measure that it transforms the subjects and the conditions from which they could emerge. Perhaps what is at stake in the pandemic is exactly that: The *an-archaeological* potency to modify, through this 'error' of nature which is COVID-19, our origin and ourselves.

---

21. Cornelius Castoriadis, *Le Monde Morcelé: Les Carrefours du Labyrinthe 3*, (Paris: Seuil, 1990), 165.

Conclusion

What happened to the future?
It will never be like before

In the end, what seems most important to us in this pandemic is its intrusive character. Indeed, it is an event that exceeds all categories of thought hitherto mobilised to understand and standardise our reality. In this perspective, while the pandemic isolates us at home, the virus inoculates our minds. Perhaps for the first time since the end of World War II and the growing monopoly of a certain *way of life* on our subjectivities, we can think of the radically new, the *in-form*, what does not yet have—and maybe never will have—form. Moreover, the pandemic revealed the historical and precarious character of what we call capitalism. Not that it equates, in itself, to the end of capitalism, as some thinkers have predicted. On the contrary, the COVID-19 pandemic could and can serve to intensify some especially authoritarian traits of the current modes of production and subjectivation: The increase in the virtualisation of human relations, the uberisation of work and the bioarztchical control of bodies and subjectivities. On the other hand, the pandemic can be read as a reaction from the planet—this is the Gaia intrusion we have already mentioned—against human parasitism, causing the flows to decrease and the air to become cleaner thanks to the closure of people in their homes. This demonstrates to lying politicians like Bolsonaro and Trump that reality does not submit to their hallucinated desires. Against Bolsonaro's 'little flu,' there is a biothanatical potency on the planet that will never be subdued. It is more likely that our species will disappear if we do not consider very carefully the few options still available. This is the great lesson that the pandemic provides.

We grew up thinking naively that one day the revolution would arrive and we would assault the capital's Winter Palace in the old-fashioned way with bayonets and singing *The Marseillaise*. Obviously, this did not happen, but somehow we are now living in a future-present in which the capitalist sensibilities are being questioned, but not overcome. It was a powerful and dangerous social experiment to have locked two billion people in their homes for an indefinite period. Most of these people could for the first time think and feel themselves, their beloved ones, their precariousness. This viral situation generates, even today, important (de)subjectivising effects against the neoliberal system. Of course, we do not disregard that there are many who cannot experience these effects. We are well aware of the unequal and unfair distribution of the risks of the pandemic, as we have already indicated several times in this book. COVID-19 is also creating a generational gap in certain countries, given that it hits the elderly with special lethality, sparing the younger ones in general. Children and adolescents, who often do not have contact with certain forms of criticism and social struggle, survive and adapt well to confinement, intensifying the virtual relationships 'lived' through the internet and many gadgets.

It is in this ambiguous dimension that the pandemic opens up as an opportunity—perhaps the last one—to rethink the configuration of our choices and institutions. Thus, what emerges from the pandemic is the evident perception that: a) we will not be back to normal; b) the neoliberal-bioarztchical 'normality' we were experiencing was never normal from an ethical point of view and must be overcome; and c) the apparatuses of centralised power and representative democracy are incapable of dealing with the crisis that they themselves have prepared. In this perspective, the idea of radical democracy can find the strait gate through which the messiah enters, in Benjamin's words.[1] New relationships with ourselves and others that do not need representation—which today is always (self)representation of the capital—are now not only possible, but necessary. What can come of it is still unknown. It is up to us to try to read the times, to bet—a fundamental gesture of the radical democracy—and to force the strait gate.[2]

More than a disease of the body, the pandemic has shown itself as a limit imposed on the thought that must be beaten. The pandemic spreads thanks to the logistics of global networks of capitalism. In this way, it has colonised affects, imposing an omnipresent fear that can

---

1. See the Thesis XVIII-B in Michael Löwy, *Fire Alarm: Reading Walter Benjamin's 'On the Concept of History,'* (New York: Verso, 2005).
2. For a radical and democratic critique of the political representantion, see: Andityas Soares de Moura Costa Matos,, *Representação Política Contra Democracia Radical: Uma Arqueologia (A)teológica do Poder Separado*, (Belo Horizonte: Fino Traço, 2019).

generate a complete worldwide reorganisation under the Hobbesian sign of (bio)security. To fight the pandemic, it is necessary—in addition to doctors, hospitals, drugs, and security measures—to reach a state of mental clarity that only a philosophy *of* life—and not simply *about* life—can constitute. It is urgent to point out the lines of escape, the biopotential dimensions of life and the forms of outbreak of a bioemergence that requires mutations, as viruses do, so that we can sur/vive. And this is so that we do not end up eliminating our unique capacities to live in the name of a supposed protection of 'Life,' currently imposed by bioarztchy. As we saw, the bioarztchy is a medical-scientific-political lifestyle that, based on the promises of the 'life specialists', sets the pace with which we must exist from now on. In this context, it seems that are violently opening the doors of a biotechnological fascism that, in the name of 'Life,' intend to snatch ours lives. It is against this that our book was written and lived.

References

Agamben, Giorgio, *Homo Sacer: Il Potere Sovrano e la Nuda Vita*, (Torino: Einaudi, 1995).

Agamben, Giorgio, 'Una Voce,' in *Quodlibet*. Available at https://www.quodlibet.it/una-voce-giorgio-agamben, accessed on 7 October 2021.

Aiewsakun, Pakorn, Katzourakis, Aris and Simmonds, Peter, 'Prisoners of War: Host Adaptation and its Constraints on Virus Evolution,' *Nature*, 17, (2019) 321-328.

Axfors, Cathrine, Contopoulos-Ioannidis, Despia G., and Ioannidis, John P. A. 'Population-level COVID-19 Mortality Risk for Non-elderly Individuals Overall and for Non-Elderly Individuals Without Underlying Diseases in Pandemic Epicenters,' *Environmental Research*, 188 (2020). Available at https://www.sciencedirect.com/science/article/pii/S0013935120307854?via%3Dihub, accessed on 7 October 2021.

Badiou, Alain, 'L'Événement 'Crise" in ed. Mercier, Antoine, *Regard sur la Crise*, (Paris: Hermann, 2010).

Badiou, Alain, 'Sur la Situation Épidémique,' in *Quartier Générale*, 26 March 2020. Available at: https://qg.media/2020/03/26/sur-la-situation-epidemique-par-alain-badiou/ accessed on 7 October 2021.

Bataille, Georges, 'The Notion of Expenditure,' in Bataille, Georges, *The Bataille Reader*, (Oxford: Blackwell, 1997) 167-181.

BBC, 'Coronavirus: Why in Germany Did the Mortality by Covid-19 be Lower than in Other Countries?,' *BBC News*, 31 March 2020. Available at: https://www.bbc.com/mundo/noticias-52111586, accessed on 7 October 2021.

Benjamin, Walter, 'Über den Begriff der Geschichte,' in Benjamin, Walter, *Gesammelte Schriften* (Frankfurt-am-Main: Suhrkamp, 1974).

Berardi, Franco 'Bifo,' 'Chronicles of the Psycho-Deflation,' in *Nero Editions.com*, 17 March 2020. Available at https://www.neroeditions.com/chronicles-of-the-psycho-deflation/, accessed on 7 October 2021.

Bichat, Xavier, *Recherches Physiologiques sur la Vie et sur la Mort* (Genève/Paris/Bruxelles: Alliance Culturelle du Livre, 1962).

Bleger, José, *Psicología de la Conducta*, (Barcelona: Paidós, 1977).

Butler, Judith, 'Capitalism has its Limits,' in *Verso Books*, 30 March 2020. Available at: https://www.versobooks.com/blogs/4603-capitalism-has-its-limits, accessed on 7 October 2021.

Campbell, Neil A., *Biology*, (California: Benjamin Cummings, 1996).

Castoriadis, Cornelius, *Le Monde Morcelé: Les Carrefours du Labyrinthe 3*, (Paris: Seuil, 1990).

Coccia, Emanuele. 'Le Virus Est Une Force Anarchique de Métamorphose,' in *Philosophie Magazine*, 26 March 2020. Available at: https://www.philomag.com/les-idees/emanuele-coccia-le-virus-est-une-force-anarchique-de-metamorphose-42893, accessed on 7 October 2021.

Corrêa, Murilo Duarte Costa, and Matos, Andityas Soares de Moura Costa. 'Viral Intrusion,' *Naked Punch*, 31 March 2020. Available at http://www.nakedpunch.com/articles/308, accessed on 7 October 2021.

Deacon, Terrence W. *Incomplete Nature: How Mind Emerged from Matter*, (New York: Norton, 2013).

Deleuze, Gilles and Guattari, Félix, *Qu'est-ce que la Philosophie?* (Paris: Les Éditions de Minuit, 1991).

Deleuze, Gilles, *Différence et Répétition*, (Paris: Presses Universitaires de France, 1968).

Deleuze, Gilles, *En medio de Spinoza*, trans. Equipo Cactus, (Buenos Aires: Cactus, 2017).

Esposito, Roberto. *Comunidad, Inmunidad y Biopolítica*, trans. Alicia García Ruiz, (Barcelona: Herder, 2009).

Esposito, Roberto. 'Curati a Oltranza,' in *Antinomie* 28, February 2020. Available at: https://antinomie.it/index.php/2020/02/28/curati-a-oltranza/, accessed on 7 October 2021.

Esposito, Roberto. 'Il Coronavirus Rafforzerà i Sovranisti.' *The Huffington Post*, 22 March 2020. Available at: https://www.huffingtonpost.it/entry/il-coronavirus-rafforzera-i-sovranisti_it_5e774fccc5b6f5b7c545fa2f, accessed on 7 October 2021.

Evans, Brad, ed. 'The Quarantine Files: Thinkers in Self-isolation.' *Los Angeles Review of Books*, 14 April 2020. Available at: https://lareviewofbooks.org/article/quarantine-files-thinkers-self-isolation/, accessed on 7 October 2021.

Fanon, Frantz. *Les Damnés de la Terre*, (Paris: Maspero, 1961).

Foucault, Michel, *Les Techniques de Soi*, in Foucault, Michel, *Dits et Écrits, Vol. II (1976-1988)*, (Paris: Gallimard (Quarto), 2001) 1602-1632.

Foucault, Michel, *Security, Territory, Population: Lectures at the Collège de France (1977-1978)*, eds. Michel Senellart and Graham Burchell, (London: Palgrave Macmillan, 2007).

Foucault, Michel, *The Government of Self and Others: Lectures at the Collège de France (1982-1983)*, ed. Arnold I. Davidson, trans. Graham Burchell, (New York: Palgrave Macmillan, 2010).

Foucault, Michel, 'Life: Experience and Science,' in Foucault, Michel, *Aesthetics, Method and Epistemology: Essential Works of Foucault (1954-1984), Vol. Two*, ed. James D. Faubion, trans. Robert Hurley, (New York: The New Press, 1998) 465-478.

Foucault, Michel. *Discipline and Punish: The Birth of the Prison*, trans. Alan Sheridan, (New York: Vintage, 1995).

Foucault, Michel. *Society Must be Defended: Lectures at the Collège de France (1975-1976)*, eds. Mauro Bertani and Alessandro Fontana, trans. David Macey, (London: Penguin, 2003).

García Collado, Francis and Matos, Andityas Soares de Moura, *Más Allá de la Biopolítica: Biopotencia, Bioarztquia, Bioemergencia*, (Girona: Documenta Universitaria, 2020).

García Collado, Francis, 'Biopolítica, Innovación y el Oxímoron de la Democracia Representativa: Autognomía y Nootrópica a las Puertas del Fascismo Biotecnológico,' in ed. Andityas Soares de Moura Costa Matos, *Ensaios de Desobediência Epistemocrítica: Dimensões Antagonistas na Era das Sujeições Bio-Político-Cibernéticas*, (Initia Via: Belo Horizonte, 2019) 39-72.

García Collado, Francis. 'Big Data y Democracia: Educación, Comunicación, Poder y Gubernamentalidad en la era de la Razón Farmacéutica,' *Astrolabio: Revista Internacional de Filosofía*, 23, (2019) 114-134.

García Collado, Francis. 'Per a què Serveix la Mort?' in eds. Capdevila, Pol and García Collado Francis, *La Modernitat de la Filosofia*, (Barcelona, La Busca, 2012) 107-121.

Garrett, Laurie, *The Coming Plague: Newly Emerging Diseases in a World Out of Balance*, (New York: Penguin, 1994).

Goldacre, Ben, *Bad Pharma: How Drug Companies Mislead Doctors and Harm Patients*, (London: Fourth Estate (HarperCollins), 2012).

Gotzsche, Peter, *Vaccines: Truth, Lies and Controversy*, (New York: Skyhorse, 2021).

Guattari, Félix, *La Revolución Molecular*, trans. Guillermo de Eugenio Pérez, (Madrid: Errata Naturae, 2017).

Guattari, Félix, *Las Tres Ecologías*, trans. José Vázquez Pérez y Umbelina Larraceleta, (Valencia, Pre-textos, 2017).

Gumbrecht, Hans Ulrich. *Unsere Breite Gegenwart*, (Berlin: Suhrkamp, 2010).

Han, Byung-Chul. 'La Emergencia Viral y el Mundo de Mañana,' *El País*, 21 March 2020. Available at: https://elpais.com/ideas/2020-03-21/la-emergencia-viral-y-el-mundo-de-manana-byung-chul-han-el-filosofo-surcoreano-que-piensa-desde-berlin.html, accessed on 7 October 2021.

Haraway, Donna, *Staying with the Trouble*, (Durham: Duke University Press, 2016).

Hardt, Michael and Negri, Antonio, *Commonwealth*, (Cambridge: Harvard University Press, 2009).

Hardt, Michael and Negri, Antonio, *Empire*, (Cambridge: Harvard University Press, 2000).

Hobbes, Thomas, *Leviathan*, (Oxford: Oxford University Press, 1965).

Huntington, Samuel P. *The Clash of Civilizations and the Remaking of World Order*, (New York: Simon & Schuster, 1996).

Ioannidis, John P. A., 'Infection Fatality Rate of COVID-19 Inferred from Seroprevalence Data.' *Bulletin of the World Health Organization*, v. 99, n. 1, pp. 19-33, 2021. Available at: https://www.ncbi.nlm.nih.gov/pmc/articles/PMC7947934/, accessed on 7 October 2021.

Klarsfeld, André and Revah, Frédéric, *Biologie de la Mort*, (Paris: Odile Jacob, 2000).

Lakoff, Andrew, *Pharmaceutical Reason*, (New York: Cambridge University Press, 2009).

Lazzarato, Maurizio, 'Sujeição e Servidão no Capitalismo Contemporâneo,' *Cadernos de Subjetividade*, 12, (2010) 168-179.

Lucretius. *De Rerum Natura/De la Naturaleza*, trans. Eduard Valentí Fiol, (Barcelona: Acantilado, 2020).

López, José Antonio, *Virus: Ni Vivos Ni Muertos*, (Córdoba: Guadalmazán, 2019).

Löwy, Michael, *Fire Alarm: Reading Walter Benjamin's 'On the Concept of History,'* (New York: Verso, 2005).

Matos, Andityas Soares de Moura Costa. *Filosofia Radical e Utopias da Inapropriabilidade: Uma Aposta An-árquica na Multidão*, (Belo Horizonte: Fino Traço, 2015).

Matos, Andityas Soares de Moura Costa. *Representação Política Contra Democracia Radical: Uma Arqueologia (A)teológica do Poder Separado*, (Belo Horizonte: Fino Traço, 2019).

Maynard Smith, John, 'The Concept of Information in Biology,' *Philosophy of Science*, 67/2 (June 2000) 177-194.

Mbembe, Achille, *Critique of Black Reason*, (Durham: Duke University Press, 2017).

Mbembe, Achille, *Necropolítica*, trans. Elisabeth F. Archambault, (Barcelona, Melusina, 2011).

Mbembe, Achille, 'Le Droit Universel à la Respiration,' in *Analyse Opinion Critique*, 4 April 2020. Available at https://aoc.media/opi

nion/2020/04/05/le-droit-universel-a-la-respiration/, accessed on 7 October 2021.

Morin, Edgar, *L'Homme et la Mort* (Paris: Seuil, 1970).

Nancy, Jean-Luc, 'Eccezione Virale' in *Antinomie*, 27 February 2020. Available at https://antinomie.it/index.php/2020/02/27/eccezione-virale/, accessed on 7 October 2021.

Pariser, Eli, *The Filter Bubble: How the New Personalised Web is Changing What We Read and How We Think*, (London: Penguin, 2011).

Phillips, Adam, *Monogamia*, trans. Daniel Najmías (Barcelona: Anagrama, 1998).

Preciado, Paul B, *Testo Junkie: Sex, Drugs, and Biopolitics in the Pharmacopornographic Era*, (New York: The Feminist Press at the City University of New York, 2008).

Preciado, Paul B., 'Aprendiendo del Vírus,' in *El País*, 27 March 2020. Available at https://elpais.com/elpais/2020/03/27/opinion/1585316952_026489.html, accessed on 7 October 2021.

Pueyo, Tomas, 'Coronavirus: The Hammer and the Dance—What the Next 18 Months Can Look Like, If Leaders Buy us Time,' *Medium*, 19 March 2020. Available at: https://medium.com/@tomaspueyo/coronavirus-the-hammer-and-the-dance-be9337092b56, accessed on 7 October 2021.

Romero Cabello, Raúl. *Microbiología Humana y Parasitología: Bases Etiológicas de las Enfermedades Infecciosas y Parasitarias*, (Madrid: Editorial Medical Panamericana, 2018).

Rose, Steven, 'Levels of Explanation in Human Behaviour: The Poverty of Evolutionary Psychology,' in Hull, David L., Regenmortel, Marc H. V. Van. eds. *Promises and Limits of Reductionism in the Biomedical Sciences* (West Sussex: John Wiley and Sons, 2002).

Said, Edward W, *Orientalism*, (New York: Pantheon, 1978).

Semerano, Giovanni, *Le Origini della Cultura Europea. Vol. II: Dizionari Etimologici. Basi Semitiche delle Lingue Indeuropee. Dizionario della Lingua Greca*, (Firenze: Leo S. Olschki, 1994).

Solé, Ricard; Elena, Santiago F., *Viruses as Complex Adaptive Systems*, (New Jersey: Princeton University Press, 2019).

Spinoza, Benedict de, *Ethics Preceded by On the Improvement of the Understanding*, ed. James Gutmann, (New York: Hafner Publishing, 1954).

Stengers, Isabelle, *Au Temps des Catastrophes: Résister à la Barbarie qui Vient* (Paris: La Découverte, 2008).

Sutter, Laurent de, "The Logistics of Pandemic,' *The Corona Crisis in Light of the Law-as-Culture Paradigm.* Available at: http://www.recht-als-kultur.de/de/aktuelles/, accessed on 7 October 2021.

Virno, Paolo, *Cuando el Verbo se Hace Carne*, trans. Eduardo Sadier (Madrid: Cactus, 2005).

Weil, Simone, 'La Personne et le Sacré' in Simone Weil, *Écrits de Londres et Dernières Lettres*, (Paris: Gallimard, 1957) 11-44.

Wolf, Maryanne, *Cómo Aprendemos a Leer*, trans. Martín Rodríguez-Courel (Barcelona: Ediciones B, 2008).

Zabala, Santiago, *Being at Large: Freedom in the Age of Alternative Facts*, (Montreal/Kingston: McGill-Queen's University Press, 2020)

Zabala, Santiago, 'Surviving Change in the Age of Alternative Facts,' *McGill-Queen's University Press*, 15 April 2020. Available at: https://www.mqup.ca/blog/surviving-change-santiago-zabala-guest-blog/, accessed on 7 October 2021.

Žižek, Slavoj, 'Coronavirus is 'Kill Bill'-esque Blow to Capitalism and Could Lead to Reinvention of Communism,' *Russia Today*, 27 February 2020. Available at: https://www.rt.com/op-ed/481831-coronavirus-kill-bill-capitalism-communism/, accessed on 7 October 2021.

About the Authors

Andityas Soares de Moura Costa Matos is Doctor in Law and Justice by the Law School of the Federal University of Minas Gerais (UFMG, Brazil). Doctor in Philosophy by the University of Coimbra (Portugal). Tenured Professor of Law Philosophy at the UFMG's Law School. Permanent Member of the Postgraduate Program in Law at the UFMG's Law School. Visiting Professor at the Barcelona University's Law School (2015-2016) and in the Cordoba University's Law School (2021-2022), both in Spain. Researcher at the Institute for Advanced Transdisciplinary Studies at UFMG (2017-2018). Researcher at several universities, such as University of Barcelona, University of Girona and University of Buenos Aires. Author of philosophical studies such as: *O Grande Sistema do Mundo: Do Pensamento Grego Originário à Mecânica Quântica* [*The Great System of the World: From Original Greek Thought to Quantum Mechanics*] (Belo Horizonte, Fino Traço, 2014), *Filosofía Radical y Utopía: Inapropiabilidad, An-arquía, A-nomía* [*Radical Philosophy and Utopia: Inappropriability, An-archy, A-nomie*] (Bogotá, Siglo del Hombre, 2015) and *Representação Política Contra Democracia Radical: Uma Arqueologia (A)teológica do Poder Separado* [*Political Representation Against Radical Democracy: An (A)theological Archeology of Separate Power*] (Belo Horizonte, Fino Traço, 2019). With Francis García Collado, is co-author of *Mas Allá de la Biopolítica: Biopotencia, Bioarztquía, Bioemergencia* (Girona, Documenta Universitaria, 2020) [*Beyond Biopolitics: Biopotency, Bioarztchy, Bioemergence*].

    vergiliopublius@hotmail.com
    andityas@ufmg.br

    https://ufmg.academia.edu/AndityasSoares
    https://periodicos.ufmg.br/index.php/revistadestrocos/

    Facebook: @estadoexcecaobrasil
    Instagram: @estadoexcecaobrasil @poesiandityas

Francis García Collado is Doctor in Philosophy by the University of Barcelona (UB, Spain). Professor of Philosophy, History of Scientific Thought and Ethics in Advertising and Public Relations in the School of Philosophy and Arts of the University of Girona (UdG). Evaluating member of the UdG Ethics and Biosafety Committee. Professor of Psychology at the School of Science and Communications at the International Universitat of Catalunya (UIC). Professor of Theory of Education in the School of Social Sciences of the Universitat of Vic—Central University of Catalunya (UVic-UCC). Professor in the Master of Neuroeducation at UVic-UCC. Professor of Ethics and Communications Psychology, Psychology and Sociology in the Superior School of Business Sciences and Public Relations (UB-ESRP). Has taught at the Centre of Human Rights of the Federal University of Goiás' Law School (UFG, Brazil) and has been visiting Professor at the Federal University of Minas Gerais (UFMG, Brazil). He is the co-coordinator of the Philosophy Conferences Cycle organized by the Barcelona Board and the Barcelona Library Consortium since 2007 and has been Professor of Philosophy at Casa Elizalde for more than fifteen years. Author of the poetry work *Grhitos [Screams]* (Barcelona, La Busca, 2012) and various philosophical essays in books published in Catalonia and Brazil. With Andityas Soares de Moura Costa Matos, is co-author of *Mas Allá de la Biopolítica: Biopotencia, Bioarztquía, Bioemergencia* (Girona, Documenta Universitaria, 2020) [*Beyond Biopolitics: Biopotency, Bioarztchy, Bioemergence*].

francisgarcia.collado@gmail.com

https://independent.academia.edu/FrancisCollado4

www.ingramcontent.com/pod-product-compliance
Lightning Source LLC
Chambersburg PA
CBHW071752080526
44588CB00013B/2220